GETTING AT THE

GETTING AT THE

Truth

Responding to Difficult
Questions about LDS Beliefs

ROBERT L. MILLET

DESERET
BOOK
SALT LAKE CITY, UTAH

Library of Congress Cataloging-in-Publication Data

Millet, Robert L.
  Getting at the truth : responding to difficult questions about LDS beliefs / Robert L. Millet.
    p. cm.
  Includes bibliographical references and index.
  ISBN 1-59038-304-4 (pbk.)
  1. Church of Jesus Christ of Latter-day Saints—Apologetic works. 2. Church of Jesus Christ of Latter-day Saints—Doctrines—Miscellanea. I. Title.
  BX8635.5.M55 2004
  289.3—dc22
                       2004001494

Printed in the United States of America   72076-075P
Publishers Printing, Salt Lake City, UT

10 9 8 7 6 5 4 3 2 1

The Standard of Truth has been erected;
no unhallowed hand can stop the work from progressing;
persecutions may rage, mobs may combine, armies may assemble,
calumny may defame, but the truth of God will go forth boldly,
nobly, and independent, till it has penetrated every continent,
visited every clime, swept every country, and sounded in every ear,
till the purposes of God shall be accomplished,
and the Great Jehovah shall say
the work is done.

—JOSEPH SMITH

CONTENTS

PREFACE

Some time ago I was sent a pamphlet about Mormonism by another religious organization that wanted to point out seeming flaws and inconsistencies of The Church of Jesus Christ of Latter-day Saints. Although a few points the authors made were interesting and fair enough, several others were blatantly false. As I turned the pages, my frustration grew, and I felt the need to respond kindly but directly to the authors of the pamphlet. They had stated that their intention was, in the words of the apostle Paul, to speak the truth in love (Ephesians 4:15), so early in my letter to them I suggested that it is much easier to state the truth *in love* when one first *states the truth!* I commented that they surely desired that any document distributed under their name be accurate in its content. To their great credit, several months later, I received a thank-you note that informed me that the pamphlet I had reviewed had since been discarded and that my comments would be incorporated into a new edition of it.

Getting at the truth is what life is all about. We spend our days and months and years striving to jettison falsehood and discover truth. We seek to rid our lives of sin and deception in order to see things as *they* really are (Jacob 4:13; D&C 93:24) rather than as *we* are. Such truth is not to be apprehended by the senses alone, nor does it come only through study. The word of the

Lord is clear: "He that keepeth [God's] commandments receiveth truth and light, until he is glorified in truth and knoweth all things" (D&C 93:28). The Prophet Joseph Smith taught similarly that saving knowledge and intelligence come only through diligence and obedience (D&C 130:19).

With the Church continuing to grow and expand, our influence is being felt more than ever before. In the process, people are beginning to recognize and acknowledge that we have no secret agenda, no private version of Mormonism, to cover up. Observers are also becoming more and more aware of the Church's stand on moral issues, our readiness to speak out and be heard on matters that threaten the home and family, and our eagerness to be involved in noble causes and humanitarian efforts.

And yet misunderstanding and misrepresentation concerning the beliefs and practices of the Latter-day Saints persist. Many millions of people throughout the earth are misguided in their views of our doctrine and our way of life. Our divine charge is "Go ye into all the world, preach the gospel to every creature, acting in the authority which I have given you, baptizing in the name of the Father, and of the Son, and of the Holy Ghost" (D&C 68:8; compare Matthew 28:19–20; Mark 16:15–18). At least a part of that charge entails answering the questions of honest truth seekers, as well as responding, when appropriate, to those who assault the faith of Latter-day Saints and attempt to dislodge the foundations of the Restoration.

This book is an effort to assist members of the Church to feel secure in their faith, to reinforce their witness and conviction, and to assure them that there are indeed answers to some of the difficult questions raised frequently by our critics. I am not authorized to speak for the Church, and so what follows are my own thoughts that have coalesced during the past thirty years as

I have searched, pondered, and prayed about challenging questions. Although I alone am responsible for the conclusions I have drawn from the evidence cited, I have endeavored to be in harmony with the standard works of the Church and the teachings of latter-day prophets and apostles.

I owe an immense debt of gratitude to many people in the preparation of this work. My assistant, Lori Soza, has, as always, borne the principal responsibility for preparing the manuscript and assisting with the arduous task of source checking. Because of the sensitive nature of much of the material contained herein, I have relied upon the editorial gifts of my editor, Suzanne Brady, of Deseret Book Company. My appreciation also extends to students and colleagues at Brigham Young University and associates of other faiths who have stretched my mind and heart and pushed me to articulate my faith more intelligibly.

The work of the Restoration is underway, and hidden treasures of eternity are coming to us through the Lord's anointed servants, line upon line, precept upon precept, here a little and there a little (Isaiah 28:10; 2 Nephi 28:30). "Therefore, fear not, little flock; do good; let earth and hell combine against you, for if ye are built upon my rock, they cannot prevail. . . . Look unto me in every thought; doubt not, fear not" (D&C 6:34, 36). God is in charge, and our trust is in him and in his powerful arm. His work will not be halted.

DON'T BE SHOCKED

The work of salvation throughout the earth will not move forward without significant opposition. As we move closer to the end of time, meaning the end of earth's temporal existence, the forces of evil will combine against the forces of good, particularly the Church of the Lamb of God. A proclamation issued in April 1845 by the Quorum of the Twelve Apostles of The Church of Jesus Christ of Latter-day Saints includes these words: "As this work progresses in its onward course, and becomes more and more an object of political and religious interest and excitement, no king, ruler, or subject, no community or individual, will stand *neutral*. All will at length be influenced by one spirit or the other; and will take sides either for or against the kingdom of God."[1]

Thus we should not be surprised when individuals or organizations take issue with teachings or practices of The Church of Jesus Christ of Latter-day Saints (hereafter, for simplicity, Church or Church of Jesus Christ). The apostle Peter wrote to the Saints scattered abroad in the meridian dispensation: "Beloved, think it not strange concerning the fiery trial which is to try you, as though some strange thing happened unto you: But rejoice, inasmuch as ye are partakers of Christ's sufferings; that, when his glory shall be revealed, ye may be glad also with exceeding joy" (1 Peter 4:12–13). We have the assurance that there will never again be an apostasy of the Lord's Church, that the kingdom of

God is here to stay, and that it will grow and expand to include hundreds of millions of people throughout the earth. Such growth, however, will not go unnoticed or unopposed.

When the priesthood was restored and the Church organized in April 1830, when missionaries were sent forth and the ordinances of salvation were reintroduced to the children of men, the winds of hatred began to blow. One bitter storm of religious wrath followed another. To the Prophet Joseph while he was in Liberty Jail, the Savior made the almost unbelievable declaration: "The ends of the earth shall inquire after thy name, and fools shall have thee in derision, and hell shall rage against thee." Then came the assurance that the sun indeed shone above the smog of sectarian hatred, for, the Lord continued, "The pure in heart, and the wise, and the noble, and the virtuous, shall seek counsel, and authority, and blessings constantly from under thy hand" (D&C 122:1–2).

"Every man to whom the heavens have been opened and who has received revelations from God has been hated by his fellows," President George Q. Cannon stated. "His life has been sought, and he has had no peace on the earth. No matter how numerous such persons have been they have been hunted and driven. So true is this that Stephen the martyr, when being stoned to death, taunted the Jews with their unbelief and the acts of their ancestors. Said he, 'which of the prophets have not your fathers persecuted? and they have slain them which showed before the coming of the Just One.'"[2]

The death of Joseph Smith did not end the bitterness that opposed him and the faithful Saints. President Spencer W. Kimball testified: "If this were not the Lord's work, the adversary would not pay any attention to us. If this Church were merely a church of men and women, teaching only the doctrines of men, we would encounter little or no criticism or resistance—

but because this is the Church of Him whose name it bears, we must not be surprised when criticism or difficulties arise."[3]

When Joseph Smith sent the first missionaries to the British Isles, the inspiration of that action was soon attested to by satanic opposition. Heber C. Kimball recounted events surrounding the first baptisms performed in that land. This incident took place in Preston, England, after it had been agreed that Elder Kimball would perform baptisms the next morning in the River Ribble, which runs through Preston.

"Sunday, July 30th (1837), about daybreak, Elder Isaac Russell (who had been appointed to preach on the obelisk in Preston Square, that day), who slept with Elder Richards in Wilfred Street, came up to the third story, where Elder Hyde and myself were sleeping, and called out, 'Brother Kimball, I want you should get up and pray for me that I may be delivered from the evil spirits that are tormenting me to such a degree that I feel I cannot live long, unless I obtain relief.'

"I had been sleeping on the back of the bed. I immediately arose, slipped off at the foot of the bed, and passed around to where he was. Elder Hyde threw his feet out, and sat up in the bed, and we laid hands on him, I being mouth, and prayed that the Lord would have mercy on him, and rebuked the devil.

"While thus engaged, I was struck with great force by some invisible power, and fell senseless on the floor. The first thing I recollected was being supported by Elder Hyde and Richards, who were praying for me; Elder Richards having followed Russell up to my room. Elders Hyde and Richards then assisted me to get on the bed, but my agony was so great I could not endure it, and I arose, bowed my knees and prayed. I then arose and sat up on the bed, when a vision was opened to our minds, and we could distinctly see the evil spirits, who foamed and gnashed their teeth at us. We gazed upon them about an hour and a half (by Willard's watch). We were not looking towards the window, but towards the wall. Space appeared before us, and we saw the devils coming in legions, with their leaders, who came within a few feet of us. They came towards us like armies rushing to battle. They appeared to be men of full stature, possessing every form and feature of men in the flesh, who were angry and desperate; and I shall never forget the vindictive malignity depicted on their countenances as they looked me in the eye; and any attempt to paint the scene which then presented itself, or portray their malice and enmity, would be vain. I perspired exceedingly, my clothes becoming as wet as if I had been taken out of the river. I felt excessive pain, and was in the greatest distress for some time. I cannot even look back on the scene without feelings of horror; yet by it I learned the power of the adversary, his enmity against the servants of God, and got some understanding of the invisible world. We distinctly heard those spirits talk and express their wrath and hellish designs against us. However, the Lord delivered us from them, and blessed us exceeding that day."

When Heber C. Kimball related this experience to Joseph Smith, he asked the Prophet what it meant, desiring to know if he and the other missionaries had done anything to cause the manifestation of evil. " 'No, Brother Heber,' he replied, 'at that time you were nigh unto the Lord; there was only a veil between you and Him, but you could not see Him. When I heard of it, it gave me great joy, for I then knew that the work of God had taken root in that land. It was this that caused the devil to make a struggle to kill you.'

"Joseph then related some of his own experience, in many contests he had had with the evil one, and said: *'The nearer a person approaches the Lord, a greater power will be manifested by the adversary to prevent the accomplishment of His purposes.'"*[4]

Since the organization of the Church in 1830, millions of people have left the various churches of Christendom to join The Church of Jesus Christ of Latter-day Saints. In so doing, they have shared a common feeling of joy and excitement about what they have found in the restored gospel. By tens and hundreds of thousands, they and their children have served as missionaries. They have gone to family and to friends to share what they have found. In the countless times that this drama has been enacted, it is hard to recall instances in which these converts have felt impelled to vilify and attack the churches they left. I know of no books written for that purpose, no movies made to that end. In the thousands of meetings I have attended, I have never heard a single sermon in which members of the Church were encouraged to fight and malign and even misrepresent persons of other faiths. By contrast, many members of the Church have had experiences with those who have chosen to leave Mormonism but who cannot then leave it alone. For these and other reasons, I have addressed here such matters as—

- how we might better understand and build stronger and more cordial relationships with our brothers and sisters of other faiths;
- how one of our greatest defenses of the faith comes simply through knowing our faith—knowing what is and what is not the doctrine of the Church, what we teach and what we do not;
- how we might respond to opposition most appropriately and peacefully;
- how we can answer a myriad of questions that come to us regularly, understand the principles that undergird those answers, and relate particulars concerning those matters;

- how we can be secure in knowing that despite what others may say or do, the work of our Lord and Master Jesus Christ will continue to grow and expand until that glorious day when "the earth shall be full of the knowledge of the Lord, as the waters cover the sea" (Isaiah 11:9).

"If we will go forward," President Gordon B. Hinckley has stated, "never losing sight of our goal, speaking ill of no one, living the great principles we know to be true, this cause will roll on in majesty and power to fill the earth."[5] He extended the calming and reassuring counsel that "we need not fear. This cause is greater than any man. It will outlast all its enemies. We need only go forward by the *power* of faith without fear."[6]

CHAPTER 1

REACHING OUT

You and I are called to be holy, to stand as lights in a darkened world, and yet we live in the world. We do not attend church every day of the week, nor do many of us associate only with persons of our own faith or moral persuasion. We have been called to come out of the world in the sense that we are to forsake the ways and whims and voices and values of the world and the worldly. Of his chosen Twelve, Jesus prayed: "I have given them thy word; and the world hath hated them, because they are not of the world, even as I am not of the world. *I pray not that thou shouldest take them out of the world, but that thou shouldest keep them from the evil*" (John 17:14–15; emphasis added).

There is a fine line here. On the one hand the Saints of the Most High are to eschew all forms of evil and reject every effort to dilute the divine or corrupt the truth, yet we are commissioned to be a leavening influence among the people of the earth. We cannot make our influence felt if we completely avoid the troublesome issues in society and isolate ourselves and our families from today's challenges. President Howard W. Hunter explained that "the gospel of Jesus Christ, which gospel we teach and the ordinances of which we perform, is a global faith with an all-embracing message. It is neither confined nor partial nor subject to history or fashion. Its essence is universally and eternally true. Its message is for all the world, restored in these latter days to meet the fundamental needs of every nation, kindred, tongue, and people on the earth. It has been established again as it was in the beginning—to build brotherhood, to preserve truth, and to save souls."[1]

As members of The Church of Jesus Christ of Latter-day Saints, we have a responsibility to love and care for our neighbors and make a difference for good in their lives. Perhaps they will join our church, but perhaps they will not. Either way, we have been charged by our Lord and Master, as well as his chosen spokesmen, to love them, to serve them, and to treat them with the same respect and kindness that we extend to persons of our own faith. Unfortunately, religious discussions with those not of our faith too often devolve into debates or wars of words as a result of defensiveness over this or that theological issue. This need not happen when men and women of goodwill talk together with an attitude of openness in a sincere effort to better understand and be understood.

In a very real sense the Latter-day Saints are a part of the larger "body of Christ," the Christian community, whether certain groups feel comfortable acknowledging our Christianity or not. Given the challenges we face in our society—fatherless homes, child and spouse abuse, divorce, poverty, increasing crime and delinquency, spiritual wickedness in high places—it seems to me foolish for men and women who claim to believe in the Lord and Savior, whose hearts and lives have been surrendered to that Savior, to allow doctrinal differences to prevent them from working together. One believes in a triune God, another believes that the Almighty is a spirit who created all things ex nihilo, and I believe that God is an exalted Man, a distinct personage and a separate God from both the Son and the Holy Ghost. Another believes that the Sabbath should be observed on Saturday; still another does not believe in blood transfusions. This one speaks in tongues, that one spends much of his time leading marches against social injustice, and a third argues that little children should be baptized. One good Baptist is a strict Calvinist; another takes freedom of the will seriously. And so on, and so on. Do we agree on the problems in our world? Do we agree that almost all of these ills have moral or spiritual roots?

President Gordon B. Hinckley pleaded with us: "We must not become disagreeable as we talk of doctrinal differences. There is no place for acrimony. But we can never surrender or compromise that knowledge which has come to us through revelation and the direct bestowal of keys and authority under the hands of those who held them anciently. Let us never forget that this is a restoration of that which was instituted by the Savior of the world. It is not a reformation of perceived false practice and doctrine that may have developed through the centuries.

"We can respect other religions and must do so. We must recognize the great good they accomplish. We must teach our children to be tolerant and friendly toward those not of our faith. We can and do work with those of other religions in the defense of those values which have made our civilization great and our society distinctive."[2]

In the spirit of Christian brotherhood and sisterhood, is it not possible to lay aside theological differences long enough to address the staggering social issues in our troubled world? My recent interactions with men and women of various faiths have had a profound effect on me. They have broadened my horizons dramatically and reminded me—a sobering reminder we all need once in a while—that we are all sons and daughters of the same Eternal Father. We may never resolve our differences on the Godhead or the Trinity, on the spiritual or corporeal nature of Deity, or on the sufficiency of the Bible, but we can agree that salvation is in Christ, that the ultimate transformation of society will come only through the application of Christian solutions to pressing moral issues, and that the regeneration of individual hearts and souls is foundational to the restoration of virtue in our communities and nations.

It is my conviction that God loves us, one and all, for I believe he is our Father in heaven and that he has tender regard for us. I also feel strongly that, despite growing wickedness, men and women throughout the earth are being led to greater light and knowledge, to the gradual realization of their own fallen nature, and thus to their need for spiritual transformation. C. S. Lewis once stated that there are people "who are slowly becoming Christians though they do not yet call themselves so. There are people who do not accept the full Christian doctrine about Christ but who are so strongly attracted by Him that they are His in a much deeper sense than they themselves understand." Lewis spoke of people "who are being led by God's secret influence to concentrate on those parts of their religion which are in agreement with Christianity, and who thus belong to Christ without knowing it."[3]

I am fully persuaded that we can be committed Latter-day Saints and that we need not compromise one whit of our doctrine or our way of life; indeed, our strength, our contribution to the religious world, lies in our distinctiveness. We are who we are, and we believe what we believe. At the same time, we can and should build bridges of friendship and understanding with those of other faiths. I believe this is what our Master would do, He who mingled with all elements of society and whose gaze penetrated the faces and the facades of this temporal world.

The people of the covenant have been charged to be "a chosen generation, a royal priesthood, an holy nation, a peculiar people; that [we] should shew forth the praises of him who hath called [us] out of darkness into his marvellous light" (1 Peter 2:9). Our religion is more than dark suits and white shirts and attending meetings, more than external trappings or successful activities. What we are, deep down to the core, is so much more important than what we are doing or what we may appear to be. Elder Bruce R. McConkie taught: "In the final analysis, the gospel of God is written, not in the dead letters of scriptural records, but in the lives of the Saints. It is not written with pen and ink on paper of man's making, but with acts and deeds in the book of life of each believing and obedient person. It is engraved in the flesh and bones and sinews of those who live a celestial law, which is the law of the gospel. It is there to be read by others, first, by those who, seeing the good works of the Saints, shall respond by glorifying our Father in heaven, and finally by the Great Judge to whom every man's life is an open book."[4]

BLESSINGS AND CHALLENGES OF REACHING OUT

In January 1991, when I was appointed dean of Religious Education at Brigham Young University, Elder Neal A. Maxwell offered me much sound counsel and repeated at least three times: "You must find ways to reach out to those not of our faith, to build bridges and friendships for the university and the Church." Those instructions rang in my ears for months. I encouraged some of our teachers of world religion classes in their desire to visit Asian countries and become personally acquainted with the people, the varying religions, and their ways of life. We broadened the reach of the Richard L. Evans Chair of Christian Understanding at BYU, and such competent and energetic scholars as David Paulsen, Darwin Thomas, Larry Porter, and Roger Keller were appointed as Evans professors. I found myself spending more and more time attending conferences, delivering lectures, and meeting religious leaders and academicians from religious schools. Concurrently, I began a reading program of books, journals, and magazines that was broad and inclusive about Christian doctrine and practice. I sensed that I would not be in a position to carry on meaningful conversations with religious leaders and scholars of other faiths if I did not understand their background, their vocabulary, and even some of the crises in their respective traditions. Since being released as dean, I have served as an Evans professor and have spent a good deal of my time in outreach, working with persons of other faiths and attempting to articulate the distinctive doctrine of the Restoration.

Unanticipated blessings have been associated with these interfaith dialogues. Some acquaintances of other faiths have become my friends. My *friends*. I have grown to appreciate them, admire them, and look up to them. On certain occasions I have felt the pure love of Christ toward them, attesting to my soul that God loves them and that what we are about is neither accident nor coincidence. I have felt the Spirit of the Lord prompting my words, shaping my expressions, and enabling me to articulate the truths of Mormonism in a manner that has taught me as well as my listeners.

I must say at this point that there is a world of difference between being able to teach the doctrines of salvation to members of our own faith and being able to do the same effectively with those not of our faith. Backgrounds and vocabularies are so different that I have been required to bend and stretch and reach for clarity of expression. Let me illustrate. It has not been uncommon for my Christian friends, particularly those who know me well and sense my commitment to the Savior, to ask me, "Bob, if you sincerely believe in the ransoming power and completed work of Jesus Christ, why do you as a people build and attend temples? Is salvation really in Christ, or must you enter the temple to be saved?" This excellent question has forced me to ponder carefully upon the place and meaning of temples in Latter-day Saint theology.

I sat at lunch a few years ago with a dear friend, Pastor Greg Johnson, who happens to be an Evangelical minister. We have met on many occasions to chat, to reflect on each other's faith, to ask hard questions, to seek to better understand. On this particular occasion, we were discussing grace and works. I had assured Greg that Latter-day Saints do believe in, accept, and rely upon the saving mercy of Jesus. "But, Bob," he said, "you folks believe you have to do so many things to be saved!"

"Like what?" I asked.

"Well," he continued, "let's just take baptism, for example. You believe that baptism is what saves you."

"No, we don't," I responded.

"Yes, you do," he followed up. "You believe baptism is essential for entrance into the celestial kingdom."

"Yes," I said, "but though baptism and other ordinances are necessary as channels of divine power and grace, they are not the things that save us. *Jesus* saves us!"

My response about baptism to my colleague is also applicable to temples and temple work. Although Latter-day Saints believe and teach that the highest form of salvation, or exaltation, comes to those who receive the blessings of the temple (D&C 131:1–4), we do not in any way believe that temple ordinances save us. Salvation is in Christ. We believe the temple makes us eligible to receive the covenants and ordinances that open the door to greater truths; it is a house of learning, of communion and inspiration, of covenants and ordinances, of service, and of personal refinement. We believe that the temple is the house of the Lord. But it is not the Lord himself. We look to Christ the Person for salvation. I doubt I would ever have come to those conclusions had I not been challenged by my friends of other faiths regarding the place of Christ in our temple worship.

Now, to be sure, there have been a host of challenges to this work of reaching out. Some have asked, "Why are you doing this? Do you really think you will convert that person to our way of thinking? How can you justify the time and expense required of such efforts?" Others are forever suspicious that anyone who wants to build relationships with us must have some malicious motive. The greatest source of frustration I have felt in this work—and the one that has brought me to the brink of turning in my badge and throwing in the towel—has not been unsuccessful encounters with other Christians but rather misunderstanding and, occasionally, outright unkindness on the part of Latter-day Saints. In some cases, I suppose, it was simply a matter of their questioning my motives or wondering how it is possible to make progress in interfaith dialogue without some form of doctrinal compromise. Too often such suspicion comes from an individual's own inability to see the bigger picture.

Another challenge with reaching out is simply being able to respond to hard questions that come from those of other faiths. Most doctrinal or historical queries can be handled easily enough. But some particularly sensitive topics—for example, that God was once a man, how Jesus is literally the Son of God, what it means for man to become like God, women and the priesthood, priesthood restriction until 1978, plural marriage, and so forth—are topics that can tax the soul, causing us to wonder how little or how much to say. Little is generally better than much, and "I really don't know" works quite well too.

One point I have begun to emphasize is that the "doctrine of the Church" today has a rather narrow focus and direction. Central and saving doctrine is what we are called upon to emphasize, rather than tangential and peripheral doctrines. Not everything that was ever spoken or written by a Church leader in the past is necessarily a part of the doctrine of the Church today. Our Church has a living, dynamic constitution, a living tree of life (D&C 1:30). We are commanded to pay heed to the words of living oracles (D&C 90:3–5).

A Broader Perspective

Reaching out requires a broader perspective on how God is working throughout the earth through men and women of all attitudes and religious persuasions. Several years ago I read the autobiography of Billy Graham, entitled *Just As I Am*.[5] It was a life-changing experience for me. I had grown up in the South watching Billy Graham crusades and thus was not completely ignorant of his prominence in the religious world. But I was not prepared for what I learned. His influence for good among rich and poor, black and white, high and low—including serving as spiritual adviser to several presidents of the United States—was almost overwhelming to me. The more I read, the more I became acquainted with a good man, a God-fearing man, a person who had felt called to take the message of Christ to the ends of the earth. I remember sitting in my chair in the living room finishing the last page of the book. No one else was home except for my wife, Shauna, who was also reading. As I laid the book down, I let out a rather loud "Wow!"

Shauna responded, "What did you say?"

I replied, "Wow! What a life!" I remember being very emotional at the time, sensing deep down that God had worked wonders through this simple and submissive North Carolina preacher.

Not long after I read the Graham autobiography, a colleague at BYU drew my attention to a general conference address given by Elder Ezra Taft Benson in April 1972: "God, the Father of us all, uses the men of the earth, especially good men, to accomplish his purposes. It has been true in the past, it is true today, it will be true in the future." Elder Benson then quoted from a conference address delivered by Elder Orson F. Whitney in 1928: "'Perhaps the Lord needs such men on the outside of His Church to help it along. They are among its auxiliaries, and can do more good for the cause where the Lord has placed them, than anywhere else. . . . Hence, some are drawn into the fold and receive a testimony of the truth; while others remain unconverted . . . the beauties and glories of the gospel being veiled temporarily from their view, for a wise purpose. The Lord will open their eyes in His own due time. *God is using more than one people for the accomplishment of His great and marvelous work. The Latter-day Saints cannot do it all.* It is too vast, too arduous for any one people.'" Elder Whitney then stated, "'We have no quarrel with those of other faiths who love the Lord. They are our partners in a certain sense.'"[6]

In June 1829 Oliver Cowdery and David Whitmer were instructed to "contend against no church, save it be the church of the devil" [D&C 18:20]. Elder B. H. Roberts offered this perceptive commentary: "I understand the injunction to Oliver Cowdery to 'contend against no church, save it be the church of the devil' [D&C 18:20], to mean that he shall contend against evil, against untruth, against all combinations of wicked men. They constitute the church of the devil, the kingdom of evil, a federation of unrighteousness; and the servants of God have a right to contend against that which is evil, let it appear where it will, in Catholic or Protestant Christendom, among the philosophical societies of deists and atheists, and even within the Church of Christ, if, unhappily, it should make its appearance there. But, *let it be understood, we are not brought necessarily into antagonism with the various sects of Christianity as such.* So far as they have retained fragments of Christian truth—and each of them has some measure of truth—that far they are acceptable unto the Lord; and it would be poor policy for us to contend against them without discrimination. Wherever we find truth, whether it exists in complete form or only in fragments, we recognize that truth as part of that sacred whole of which the Church of Jesus Christ is the custodian; and I repeat that our relationship to the religious world is not one that calls for the denunciation of sectarian churches as composing the church of the devil."

Continuing, Elder Roberts demonstrates the breadth necessary in reaching out to understand our brothers and sisters of other faiths: "All that makes for untruth, for unrighteousness constitutes the kingdom of evil—the church of the devil. *All that makes for truth, for righteousness, is of God;* it constitutes the kingdom of righteousness—the empire of Jehovah; and, in a certain sense at least, constitutes the Church of Christ. With the latter—the kingdom of righteousness—we have no warfare. On the contrary both the spirit of the Lord's commandments to His servants and the dictates of right reason would suggest that we seek to enlarge this kingdom of righteousness both by recognizing such truths as it possesses and seeking the friendship and cooperation of the righteous men and women who constitute its membership."[7]

Let me pose three questions that I believe we have not pondered enough. What was the Great Apostasy? What was lost? What was *not* lost? We know from the Book of Mormon and from modern scripture that after the gospel was delivered to the Gentiles, plain and precious truths, as well as many covenants of the Lord, were taken from, or kept back, from the Bible and from the gospel of Jesus Christ (1 Nephi 13; D&C 6:26; 8:11;

Moses 1:40–41). We know that with the deaths of the apostles the keys of the kingdom of God—the directing power, the right of presidency—were lost. Those apostolic keys had been conferred to direct the work of the ministry (including overseeing and performing the ordinances, or sacraments) and also to assure the correctness of doctrine and practice within and between the branches of the Church. The truths and covenants that were lost surely included the teachings and ordinances of the temple and the nature of exaltation, the destiny of man (including his premortal existence), the nature and personality of God and the Godhead, life and labors in the postmortal spirit world, three degrees of glory in the heavens hereafter, and so forth.

Over the centuries, in an effort to satisfy the accusations of Jews who denounced the notion of three Gods (Father, Son, and Holy Ghost) as polytheistic and at the same time incorporate ancient but appealing Greek philosophical concepts of an all-powerful moving force in the universe, the Christian Church began to redefine the Father, the Son, and the Holy Spirit. Debate on the nature of the Godhead took place at Nicaea (325), Constantinople (381), Ephesus (431), and Chalcedon (451), resulting in creedal statements that became the walk and talk of Christian doctrine. Men sought to harmonize revealed doctrine with Greek philosophy and Judaic monotheism, which resulted in the corruption of fundamental and foundational truths.

What is the result? As one writer not of our faith has observed: "The classical theological tradition became misguided when, under the influence of Hellenistic philosophy, it defined God's perfection in static, timeless terms. All change was considered an imperfection and thus not applicable to God."[8] Further, "since Plato, Western philosophy has been infatuated with the idea of an unchanging, timeless reality. Time and all change were considered less real and less good than the unchanging timeless realm. . . . This infatuation with the 'unchanging' unfortunately crept into the church early on and has colored the way Christians look at the world, read their Bibles, and develop their theology."[9]

I have wrestled for years with the meaning of certain verses in the Book of Mormon. The allegory of Zenos (Jacob 5) seems to divide the history of the world (and of God's patient workings with his covenant people) into distinct time periods. My understanding is that beginning in verse 29, after "a long time had passed away," we have moved through a universal apostasy into the dispensation of the fulness of times. Verses 29 through 77 are thus devoted principally to God's dealings with the posterity of Jacob from the time of the call of Joseph Smith until the end of the Millennium. After the Lord of the vineyard and his servant return to the mother tree, they discover that it has produced wild fruit, "and there is none of it which is good" (v. 32). This language is reminiscent of what Joseph Smith learned in the First Vision: "I was answered that I must join none of them [the churches of his day], for they were all wrong" (Joseph Smith–History 1:19).

Returning to the allegory of Zenos, we read that the Lord of the vineyard asks what should be done to the tree to produce and preserve good fruit. The servant answers: "Behold, because thou didst graft in the branches of the wild olive-tree they have nourished the roots, that they are alive and they have not perished; wherefore thou beholdest that they are yet good" (Jacob 5:34). What are the roots that are alive and "yet good"? When I first arrived at BYU, one of the senior faculty commented that he believed the roots were the blood of Israel. There is much to recommend this idea, and yet I would like to suggest another, perhaps related, interpretation. What if the roots are remnants of

Christianity, pieces and parts and principles of the original gospel of Jesus Christ that have survived the centuries through the teachings or practices of both Protestant and Catholic churches? It is as though the servant were saying to his Master: "Look, we have a foundation upon which to build, an ancient archetype of the full gospel that rests deep within the souls and minds of good people throughout the earth. We can begin the final work of gathering Israel, can restore and replace and rebuild upon those fundamental verities of the primitive gospel." Having discussed the passing of the primitive Church and the flickering and dimming (but not dousing) of the flame of Christian faith, President Boyd K. Packer stated: "But always, as it had from the beginning, the Spirit of God inspired worthy souls. We owe an immense debt to the protesters and the reformers who preserved the scriptures and translated them. They knew something had been lost. They kept the flame alive as best they could."[10]

It is reasonable, therefore, that elements of truth, pieces of a much larger mosaic, should be found throughout the world in varying cultures and among diverse religious groups. Further, as the world has passed through phases of apostasy and restoration, relics of revealed doctrine remain, albeit in some cases in altered or even convoluted forms. President Joseph F. Smith had much to say to those who seek to upstage Christianity. Jesus Christ, he taught, "being the fountain of truth, is no imitator. He taught the truth first; it was his before it was given to man.

" . . . If we find truth in broken fragments through the ages, it may be set down as an incontrovertible fact that it originated at the fountain, and was given to philosophers, inventors, patriots, reformers, and prophets by the inspiration of God. It came from him through his Son Jesus Christ and the Holy Ghost, in the first place, and from no other source. It is eternal."[11]

Not long ago, as part of my personal scripture study early

one morning, I found myself reading Doctrine and Covenants 10, the section that includes instructions to the young Prophet Joseph Smith regarding the loss of the 116 manuscript pages of the Book of Mormon. Toward the end of the revelation, the Lord speaks of the prayers of the ancient Nephites that the fulness of the gospel might be made known in a future day to people who would come to America and that this land "might be free unto all of whatsoever nation, kindred, tongue, or people they may be. And now, behold, according to their faith in their prayers will I bring this part of my gospel [specifically the Book of Mormon but also the other revelations of the Restoration] to the knowledge of my people. Behold, I do not bring it to destroy that which they have received, but to build it up" (D&C 10:51–52).

This seems to be the Lord's way of affirming that when he delivers additional light and truth to his children, even additional scripture, he in no way detracts from what has been dispensed before. In this case, neither the Book of Mormon nor additional revelations would lessen in the slightest the precious and distinctive contribution of the Holy Bible. In truth, the scriptures of the Restoration bear witness with the Bible of the divinity of Jesus Christ and, working together, these books of scripture confound false doctrine, lay down contention, and establish peace (2 Nephi 3:12).

Section 10 continues: "And for this cause have I said: If this generation harden not their hearts, I will establish my church among them. *Now I do not say this to destroy my church, but I say this to build up my church*" (D&C 10:53–54; emphasis added). In the summer of 1828, almost two years before Joseph Smith and the early Saints gathered at Father Whitmer's home to organize the Church of Christ, the Lord seems to be saying, "I do not speak concerning the coming organization of the restored

Church in order to destroy my church, but I say this to build up my church."

What was his church in the summer of 1828? The restored Church, equipped with doctrine and scripture and divine authority was not yet on earth. I suggest that when the Lord in section 10 refers to "my church," he may be referring to Christianity in general, to the Christian world, to Christendom. That idea is in harmony with Elder B. H. Roberts's statement that "all that makes for truth, for righteousness, is of God; it constitutes the kingdom of righteousness—the empire of Jehovah; and, in a certain sense at least, constitutes the Church of Christ."[12] In short, while we as Latter-day Saints claim to have received angelic ministrations and divine authority, are neither Catholic nor Protestant, and thus stand independent in the religious world, we are part of a larger whole—we are what might be called "Christian, but different." We really need to try to view things through those lenses if we are to become effective in reaching out to those of other faiths.

RELATING TO THOSE WITH DIFFERENCES

I am immeasurably grateful for the fulness of the gospel—for the priesthood, for living apostles and prophets, for the ordinances of salvation, for temples and sealing powers, and for mind-expanding and liberating doctrines. But as I look more and more often into the eyes of persons of other faiths, sensing their goodness, perceiving their commitment to God, and feeling those quiet, profound impressions bearing witness to my soul, I have received an expanding awareness that God knows them, loves them, and desires for me to love, respect, and better understand them. Far too often we allow doctrinal differences to deter us from fruitful conversation, enlightening discussion, and joint participation in moral causes. This must not be.

I believe with all my heart in God and in his Son, Jesus Christ. I am committed to the doctrine and practices of The Church of Jesus Christ of Latter-day Saints; indeed, I have never been more committed to my own religious faith than I am right now. At the same time, I have never been more liberal in my views—in the proper sense of the word *liberal,* meaning "open, receptive"—to people of other faiths, especially Christian faiths. To some extent I am motivated in this direction by a statement of the prophet Mormon: "For behold, the Spirit of Christ is given to every man, that he may know good from evil; wherefore, I show unto you the way to judge; for everything which inviteth to do good, and to persuade to believe in Christ, is sent forth by the power and gift of Christ; wherefore ye may know with a perfect knowledge it is of God" (Moroni 7:16).

So often people of different religious persuasions simply talk past one another when they converse on matters religious. They may use the same words, but they bring different mindsets and entirely different perspectives to the conversation. In other situations individuals employ different vocabularies but intend to convey the same message. Confusion, misunderstanding, and misrepresentation inevitably follow. If there is anything needed in this confused world, it is understanding. Although as Latter-day Saints we readily acknowledge that not all who learn of our doctrine will accept what we teach, it is very important to us that others *understand* what we say and what we mean. Elder Neal A. Maxwell counseled, "It is important in our relationships with our fellowmen that we approach them as neighbors and as brothers and sisters rather than coming at them flinging theological thunderbolts."[13]

Reaching out is not debate. Reaching out is not ecumenism. Reaching out is not being timid to teach or hesitant to herald the message of the Restoration. Reaching out entails neither compromise nor concession. Friendliness with others does not preclude firmness in our faith. A sad and unfortunate incident highlights the need for us as Latter-day Saints to broaden ourselves out as a people and open our hearts to the Spirit of Christ more often. My friend Greg Johnson, who is a Baptist pastor, shared with me a letter he wrote recently to school administrators responsible for the school where his daughter Indiana attends first grade in a predominantly LDS community:

"Several times this new school year," he writes, "as well as a time or two last year, she has experienced some difficulties because on occasion she wears a cross necklace to school. As an Evangelical Christian family, it is appropriate in our tradition of faith to wear the symbol of a cross as jewelry as a reminder of the wonderful gift we receive because of the death, burial, and resurrection of Jesus Christ. She received her necklace as a gift from a relative and loves to wear it. As a family, we have discussed the symbol of the cross, and she can tell anyone who asks her why she wears it what it means to her.

"The difficulty she has experienced . . . is that some children in her class have told her that it is bad to wear the cross. One child even said that he hated the cross and that she should take it off. These experiences, as you might understand, have been confusing to her and we have done our best to explain to her that we believe the cross to be a wonderful symbol of her faith and that it is not wrong for her to wear it if she wants to, which she does. As a parent, I shared these matters with our school's principal and she invited me to share my concerns with the parents of [the school district] in this newsletter. I would simply petition each parent to take a few moments with their children to explain to them that in a public school there will obviously be children with a wide range of spiritual beliefs and that we need to respect the faith of others. Children of all faiths should have the freedom to live out their beliefs without facing challenges or insults. My hope is that such an exercise of communication would make our community a better place to live in, a place of understanding and respect for all."

To reach out is to comply with what Elder M. Russell Ballard called the "doctrine of inclusion." "Our doctrines and beliefs are important to us," he taught. "We embrace them and cherish them. I am not suggesting for a moment that we shouldn't. On the contrary, our peculiarity and the uniqueness of the message of the restored gospel of Jesus Christ are indispensable elements in offering the people of the world a clear choice. Neither am I suggesting that we should associate in any relationship that would place us or our families at spiritual risk." Quoting the First Presidency, Elder Ballard reaffirmed: " 'Our message . . . is one of special love and concern for the eternal welfare of all men and women, regardless of religious belief, race, or nationality, knowing that we are truly brothers and sisters of the same Eternal Father' (First Presidency statement, 15 Feb. 1978).

"That is our doctrine—a doctrine of inclusion. That is what we believe. That is what we have been taught. Of all people on this earth, we should be the most loving, the kindest, and the most tolerant because of that doctrine."[14]

"Disagreeing with one another need not, and should not, be scary and divisive," Christian scholar Gregory Boyd has written, "so long as we keep our hearts and minds focused on the person of Jesus Christ. Indeed, when our hearts and minds are properly focused, our dialogues with one another, however impassioned they may be, become the means by which we lovingly help each other appreciate aspects of God's Word we might otherwise overlook or fail to understand."[15] We can possess what my friend Richard Mouw, president of Fuller Theological Seminary, calls "convicted civility"—that is, we can be completely committed to our own faith and way of life but also be eager to learn and grow in understanding and thus to treat those with differing views with the dignity and respect they deserve as sons or daughters of God.[16] Following are several thought-provoking statements from Richard Mouw's book *Uncommon Decency: Christian Civility in an Uncivil World:*

"As Martin Marty has observed, one of the real problems in modern life is that the people who are good at being civil often lack strong convictions and people who have strong convictions often lack civility" (12).

"Christians need to be careful about seeing civility as a mere strategy for evangelism. As an evangelical Christian I want to be careful not to be misunderstood as I make this point. I want people to accept the evangel, the good news of salvation through Jesus Christ. I place a high priority on the evangelistic task. But this does not mean that Christian civility is simply an evangelistic ploy—being nice to people merely because we want them to become Christians" (28).

"When we approach others in a civil manner, we must listen carefully to them. Even when we strongly disagree with their basic perspectives, we must be open to the possibility that they will help us discern the truth more clearly. Being a civil Christian means being open to God's surprises" (67).

"[We need] to have such a total trust in Christ that we are not afraid to follow the truth wherever it leads us. He is 'the true light, which enlightens everyone' (Jn 1:9). Jesus is *the* Truth. We do not have to be afraid, then, to enter into dialog with people from other religious traditions. If we find truth in what they say, we must step out in faith to reach for it—Jesus' arms will be there to catch us!" (106).

President Gordon B. Hinckley said of the Latter-day Saints: "We want to be good neighbors; we want to be good friends.

We feel we can differ theologically with people without being disagreeable in any sense. We hope they feel the same way toward us. We have many friends and many associations with people who are not of our faith, with whom we deal constantly, and we have a wonderful relationship. It disturbs me when I hear about any antagonisms. . . . I don't think they are necessary. I hope that we can overcome them."[17]

Consider other comments from President Hinckley:

"Let us be good citizens of the nations in which we live. Let us be good neighbors in our communities. Let us acknowledge the diversity of our society, recognizing the good in all people. We need not make any surrender of our theology. But we can set aside any element of suspicion, of provincialism, of parochialism."[18]

"We are met to worship the Lord, to declare His divinity and His living reality. We are met to reaffirm our love for Him and our knowledge of His love for us. No one, regardless of what he or she may say, can diminish that love.

"There are some who try. For instance, there are some of other faiths who do not regard us as Christians. That is not important. How we regard ourselves is what is important. We acknowledge without hesitation that there are differences between us. Were this not so, there would have been no need for a restoration of the gospel. . . .

"I hope we do not argue over this matter. There is no reason to debate it. We simply, quietly, and without apology testify that God has revealed himself and his Beloved Son in opening this full and final dispensation of his work."[19]

"Now, brethren and sisters, let us return to our homes with resolution in our hearts to do a little better than we have done in the past. We can all be a little kinder, a little more generous, a little more thoughtful of one another. We can be a little more tolerant and friendly to those not of our faith, going out of our way to show our respect for them. We cannot afford to be arrogant or self-righteous. It is our obligation to reach out in helpfulness, not only to our own but to all others as well. Their interest in and respect for this Church will increase as we do so."[20]

"Our membership has grown. I believe it has grown in faithfulness. . . . Those who observe us say that we are moving into the mainstream of religion. We are not changing. The world's perception of us is changing. We teach the same doctrine. We have the same organization. We labor to perform the same good works. But the old hatred is disappearing; the old persecution is dying. People are better informed. They are coming to realize what we stand for and what we do."[21]

President Brigham Young explained that "we, the Latter-day Saints, take the liberty of believing more than our Christian brethren: we not only believe . . . the Bible, but . . . the whole of the plan of salvation that Jesus has given to us. Do we differ from others who believe in the Lord Jesus Christ? No, only in believing more."[22] It is, of course, the "more" that makes many in the Christian world very nervous and usually suspicious of us. But it is the "more" that allows us to make a meaningful contribution in the religious world.

CONCLUSION

The older I get, the less prone I am to believe in coincidence. I believe that God has a divine plan not only for the ultimate establishment of the kingdom of God on earth but also an individualized plan for each one of us. I gladly and eagerly acknowledge his hand in all things, including the orchestration of events in our lives and the interlacing of our daily associations. I believe he brings people into our paths who can bless and enlighten us, and I know that he brings us into contact with people whose acquaintance will, down the road, open doors, dissolve barriers, and make strait the way of the Lord. The prayer of Elisha for the young lad seems particularly pertinent to our work: "Lord, I pray thee, open [our] eyes, that [we] may see" (2 Kings 6:17).

Joseph Smith observed: "While one portion of the human race is judging and condemning the other without mercy, the Great Parent of the universe looks upon the whole of the human family with a fatherly care and paternal regard; He views them as His offspring, and without any of those contracted feelings that influence the children of men, causes 'His sun to rise on the evil and on the good, and sendeth rain on the just and on the unjust.' He holds the reins of judgment in His hands; He is a wise Lawgiver, and will judge all men, not according to the narrow, contracted notions of men, but 'according to the deeds done in the body whether they be good or evil.'"[23] Thus our charge, in the words of President Howard W. Hunter, is to "seek to enlarge the circle of love and understanding among all the people of the earth."[24]

CHAPTER 2

How We Know

I listened with much interest as four children in my home ward bore their testimonies in turn. The first spoke with the confidence we might expect from a seasoned adult member of the Church. She said, essentially, "I want to bear my testimony that I know that the Church is true, that Joseph Smith was a prophet of God, and that President Gordon B. Hinckley is our living prophet today." She then shared some personal feelings and sat down. I pondered on her words, on the depth of sincerity evident in her voice, and wondered: *Does* she know? Does she *really* know? How much *could* she know?

I reflected on the experience again and again during the day. It was affirmed to my mind and heart that little children can know the things of God by the power of the Spirit of God (1 Corinthians 2:11–14) and can speak words of truth and wisdom, just as their adult counterparts can (Alma 32:23). A testimony is not something you either have or do not have. Rather, it is an impression of the Spirit about the truthfulness of eternal things, an inner awareness that ranges along a spiritual continuum from a simple peaceful feeling to a perfect knowledge.

It has wisely been observed that the strength of our Church lies not alone in the powerful witnesses of the fifteen men we sustain as prophets, seers, and revelators but also in the deep assurance and resolve that rest in the souls of individual Saints of the

Most High, from Alaska to Zanzibar. A testimony may begin through trusting in the witness of another, of one who knows for sure; indeed, to believe on the faith of one who knows is a spiritual gift, a gift that can lead to eternal life (D&C 46:13–14). And yet surely each of us desires to possess our own witness, an independent knowledge of the reality of God our Father, the redemptive mission of Jesus the Christ, and the divine call of Joseph Smith and the work of the Restoration. President Heber C. Kimball warned us of a test to come, a test that would separate out those who profess membership in the Church but do not possess a personal, living testimony sufficient to see them through hard times. "The time will come when no man nor woman will be able to endure on borrowed light," he said. "Each will have to be guided by the light within himself. If you do not have it, how can you stand?"[1]

FAITH IN THE UNSEEN

A few years ago a Baptist minister friend and I were driving through Boston to the LDS Institute of Religion at Cambridge. As is my custom nearly every time I have been there, I became absolutely lost. We stopped several times for directions, and each helpful person would point us the way and say with much assurance, "You can't miss it." After having heard that phrase five or six times, I asked our seventh helper for directions, beginning with, "Please don't say we can't miss it, because I assure you we can. We have done it again and again."

During this scavenger hunt of sorts, my colleague and I visited. He commented on a matter that we had discussed several times, namely the idea that Latter-day Saints are more prone to rely upon feelings than tangible evidence for truth of religious claims.

I responded, "Do you believe in the literal bodily resurrection of Jesus Christ?"

The look he gave me was similar to the look a sixteen-year-old would give someone who had asked what the teenager felt to be an inane question. "Of course I believe in the resurrection, Bob; I'm an ordained minister."

"But why do you believe in the resurrection? How do you know it really happened?"

He answered, "Because the New Testament teaches of the resurrection of Jesus."

I shot right back, "But how do you know that the New Testament accounts are true? How do you know the Bible can be trusted? Maybe someone just made all of this up. Maybe the Bible is a giant hoax."

"No," he said, "there is strong evidence to support the truthfulness of the Bible."

"Like what?"

"Well, there are archaeological, historical, and cultural evidences that what is being described actually happened."

I then asked, "And so that's how you know the resurrection is real?"

"I suppose so," he said.

My mind raced, and I said something I hadn't planned to say. "You know, I feel a great sense of sadness right now."

My Evangelical friend was surprised. "Sadness? Why are you sad?"

"I was just thinking of a good friend of mine, an older woman in Montgomery, Alabama," I replied.

"What about her?"

I said, "I was thinking of how sad it is that this wonderful and devoted Christian, a person who has given her life to Jesus and cherished and memorized Bible passages like few people I know, a woman whose life manifests her complete commitment to the Savior, is not really entitled to have a witness of the truthfulness of the Bible."

"Why is that?" he asked.

"Well, she knows precious little about archaeology or languages or culture or history or manuscripts, so I suppose she can't know within her heart that the Bible really is the word of God."

"Of course she can," he said. "She can have her faith, her personal witness that the Bible is true."

I pulled off to the side of the road and stopped the car. I turned to him, smiled, and said, "Do you mean that the power of the Holy Spirit can testify to her soul that her Bible is completely trustworthy and can be relied upon as God's word?"

"Yes, that's what I mean."

My smile broadened as I added, "Then we've come full circle."

"What do you mean by that?" he asked.

I answered, "You're telling me that this good woman, one who has none of the supposed requisite background or knowledge of external evidence, can have a witness of the Spirit, including deep personal feelings about the Bible, and that those feelings are genuine and heaven-sent."

My friend looked into my eyes and smiled. "I see where you're going with this."

What followed was one of the most productive conversations of our time as friends. We agreed that it is so easy to yield to the temptation to categorize and pigeonhole and stereotype persons whose faith is different from our own. It is so easy to overstate, to misrepresent, to create and then dismantle "straw men" in an effort to establish our own point.

We agreed that Evangelical Christians and Latter-day Saint

Christians both base their faith upon evidence—both seen and unseen. Although saving faith is always built upon that which is true, upon an actual historical moment in time, upon something that really existed in the past, true believers will never allow their faith to be held hostage by what science has or has not found at a given time. I know, for example, that Jesus fed the five thousand, healed the sick, raised the dead, calmed the storm, and rose from the dead. I know all of that, not because I have physical evidence for each of those miraculous events (because I do not), nor even because I can read of these things in the New Testament, which I accept with all my heart. I know these things actually happened because the Spirit of the Living God bears witness to my spirit that the Lord of Life did all the scriptures say he did, and more.

A prominent historian of religion, Randall Balmer, has written: "I believe because of the epiphanies, small and large, that have intersected my path—small, discrete moments of grace when I have sensed a kind of superintending presence outside of myself. I believe because these moments . . . are too precious to discard, and I choose not to trivialize them by reducing them to rational explanation. I believe because, for me, the alternative to belief is far too daunting. I believe because, at the turn of the twenty-first century, belief itself is an act of defiance in a society still enthralled by the blandishments of Enlightenment rationalism. . . .

"Somehow, I don't think Jeffrey [who asks how he can know there is a God] wants me to rehearse the ontological, the teleological, and the cosmological arguments for the existence of God. . . . So instead of dusting off the teleological argument, I think I'll remind Jeffrey about Karl Barth, arguably the most important theologian of the twentieth century. Toward the end of his life, after he had written volume after volume on the transcendence of God and the centrality of Jesus, Barth was asked to sum up his work. The good doctor paused for a minute and no doubt looked out the window and played with the stubble on his chin before responding with the words of a Sunday school ditty: 'Jesus loves me, this I know, for the Bible tells me so.'"[2]

Many years ago on a Sunday morning I opened the door and reached down to pick up the morning newspaper. Beside the paper lay a plastic bag containing a paperback book. On the cover was a lovely picture of a mountain stream, but the title of the book told me what the book was all about—it was an anti-Mormon treatise. I browsed through the book, observing that many of its arguments against The Church of Jesus Christ of Latter-day Saints were old and worn-out ones, dead horses that have been beaten since the days of E. D. Howe. Latter-day Saints had responded to the issues posed scores of times, but the issues continued to crop up. Nonetheless, one section of the book did prove to be of some interest to me. In essence, the author pointed out that eventually two Mormon missionaries would come to the reader's door. If they do come, he pleaded, don't let them in. If, however, you do let them in, then don't listen to them. If they are allowed to tell you about their message, about Joseph Smith and angels and golden plates, they will ask you to kneel and pray about the truthfulness of these things. Whatever you do, don't pray! The writer then made this unusual observation: In ascertaining the truthfulness of a religious claim, there are three things a person can never trust: his thoughts, his feelings; and his prayers. I was all ears at this point, wondering how we could ever know anything. I didn't have to wait long, for the writer then noted that the only thing that could be trusted was the Holy Bible itself.

I shook my head and felt deep sadness for the author. How

could a person know of the truthfulness even of the Bible if he or she could not think, feel, or pray? I experienced a tumult of feelings at that moment. It was obvious that the writer could not see the blatant inconsistency and irrationality of his own words. I tried to put myself into the place of a reader who was not a Latter-day Saint and wondered how I might feel upon reading such things. To be honest, I would feel insulted that I could not be trusted enough in my pursuit of truth to rely upon my mind, my heart, or even the most tried and true method of obtaining divine direction—prayer itself.

My friend and colleague Craig Blomberg once observed: "It's ironic: The Bible considers it praiseworthy to have a faith that does not require evidence. Remember how Jesus replied to doubting Thomas: 'You believe because you see; blessed are those who have not seen and yet believe.' And I know evidence can never compel or coerce faith. We cannot supplant the role of the Holy Spirit, which is often a concern of Christians when they hear discussions of this kind.

"But I'll tell you this: there are plenty of stories of scholars in the New Testament field who have not been Christians, yet through their study of these very issues have come to faith in Christ. And there have been countless more scholars, already believers, whose faith has been made stronger, more solid, more grounded, because of the evidence—and that's the category I fall into."[3]

True believers will always be challenged by those who refuse to see. In a very real sense, believing is seeing. No member of the Church need feel embarrassed at being unable to produce the golden plates or the complete Egyptian papyrus. No member of the Church should hesitate to bear testimony of verities that remain in the realm of faith, that are seen only with the eyes of faith. Elder Neal A. Maxwell has written: "It is the author's opinion that all the scriptures, including the Book of Mormon, will remain in the realm of faith. Science will not be able to prove or disprove holy writ. However, enough plausible evidence will come forth to prevent scoffers from having a field day, but not enough to remove the requirement of faith. Believers must be patient during such unfolding."[4]

Similarly, President Ezra Taft Benson pointed out: "We do not have to prove the Book of Mormon is true. The book is its own proof. All we need to do is read it and declare it. The Book of Mormon is not on trial—the people of the world, including the members of the Church, are on trial as to what they will do with this second witness for Christ."[5]

"We are not required to prove that the Book of Mormon is true or is an authentic record through external evidences—though there are many. It never has been the case, nor is it so now, that the studies of the learned will prove the Book or Mormon true or false. The origin, preparation, translation, and verification of the truth of the Book of Mormon have all been retained in the hands of the Lord, and the Lord makes no mistakes. You can be assured of that."[6]

President Gordon B. Hinckley put things in proper perspective when he taught: "I can hold [the Book of Mormon] in my hand. It is real. It has weight and substance that can be physically measured. I can open its pages and read, and it has language both beautiful and uplifting. The ancient record from which it was translated came out of the earth as a voice speaking from the dust. . . .

"The evidence for its truth, for its validity in a world that is prone to demand evidence, lies not in archaeology or anthropology, though these may be helpful to some. It lies not in word research or historical analysis, though these may be confirmatory. The evidence for its truth and validity lies within the covers of the book itself. The test of its truth lies in reading it. It is a book of God. Reasonable individuals may sincerely question its origin, but those who read it prayerfully may come to know by a power beyond their natural senses that it is true, that it contains the word of God, that it outlines saving truths of the everlasting gospel, that it came forth by the gift and power of God."[7]

Though we seek to make friends and build bridges of understanding where possible, we do not court favor, concede, or compromise one whit on what we believe. Some doctrines, such as the doctrine of the "only true and living church" (D&C 1:30), by their very nature, arouse antagonism in those of other faiths. Would it not be wise to avoid, or at least downplay, such divisive points? Perhaps, some say, we should focus on matters we have in common and put aside, for the time being, the distinctive teachings of the Restoration. Elder Boyd K. Packer declared: "If we thought only in terms of diplomacy or popularity, surely we should change our course. But we must hold tightly to it even though some turn away. . . .

"It is not an easy thing for us to defend the position that bothers so many others.

"Brethren and sisters, never be ashamed of the gospel of Jesus Christ. Never apologize for the sacred doctrines of the gospel. Never feel inadequate and unsettled because you cannot explain them to the satisfaction of all who might inquire of you.

"Do not be ill at ease or uncomfortable because you can give little more than your conviction. . . .

"If we can stand without shame, without hesitancy, without embarrassment, without reservation to bear witness that the gospel has been restored, that there are prophets and Apostles upon the earth, that the truth is available for all mankind, the Lord's Spirit will be with us. And that assurance can be affirmed to others."[8]

TRUTH AND SIGNIFICANCE

In the end, the only way that the things of God can be known is by the power of the Holy Ghost. These things are what the scriptures call the "mysteries of God." The only way spiritual truths may be known is by the quiet whisperings of the Holy Ghost. How did Alma the Younger know? Was it because he was struck to the ground by an angel? Was it because he lay immobile and speechless for three days while he underwent a confrontation with himself and his sinful and rebellious past? No, Alma knew as we know. He may have undergone a serious turnaround in his life through the intervention of a heavenly messenger, but the witness that drove and directed this magnificent convert was the witness of the Spirit. In his own words, "Behold, I testify unto you that I do know that these things whereof I have spoken are true. And how do ye suppose that I know of their surety? Behold, I say unto you *they are made known unto me by the Holy Spirit of God.* Behold, I have fasted and prayed many days that I might know these things of myself. And now I do know of myself that they are true; for the Lord God hath made them manifest unto me by his Holy Spirit; and this is the spirit of revelation which is in me" (Alma 5:45–46; emphasis added).

On the other hand, we can sense the *significance* of a spiritual reality by the loud janglings of opposition it engenders. For example, what do the following locations have in common: Portland, Dallas, Atlanta, White Plains, Nashville, Denver, Stockholm, and Ghana? In each of these places the announcement that a Latter-day Saint temple was to be built there brought opponents and even zealots out of the woodwork. As President Brigham Young once said: "Some say, '. . . we never began to build a temple without the bells of hell beginning to ring.' I want to hear them ring again."[9]

If I did not already know by the quiet whisperings of the Spirit within me that what goes on within temples is true and is of eternal import, I would likely recognize the significance of the temple by the opposition that seems almost to flow naturally from those who refuse to see.

Consider another illustration. Why do so many people throughout the world write scathing books, deliver biting addresses, and prepare vicious videos denouncing the Book of Mormon? What is it about words in black type on a white page, all of which are uplifting and edifying, that invite men and women to come unto Christ and be perfected in him, that would arouse such bitter antagonism? Once again, if I did not already know by the quiet whisperings of the Spirit that the Book of Mormon is truly heaven-sent and indeed Another Testament of Jesus Christ, I would recognize its significance—its power to settle doctrinal disputes, touch hearts, and transform men and women's lives—by the loud and hostile reactions people tend to have toward it.

Hugh Nibley, one of the greatest minds of this dispensation, a defender of the faith throughout his life, stated: "The words of the prophets cannot be held to the tentative and defective tests that men have devised for them. Science, philosophy, and common sense all have a right to their day in court. But the last word does not lie with them. Every time men in their wisdom have come forth with the last word, other words have promptly followed. The last word is a testimony of the gospel that comes only by direct revelation. Our Father in heaven speaks it, and if it were in perfect agreement with the science of today, it would surely be out of line with the science of tomorrow. Let us not, therefore, seek to hold God to the learned opinions of the moment when he speaks the language of eternity."[10]

CONCLUSION

I have learned a few things as I have learned a few things over the years. I thank God for the formal education I have received, for the privilege it is (and I count it such) to have received university training and to have earned bachelor's, master's, and doctoral degrees. Education has expanded my mind and opened conversations and doors for me. It has taught me what books to read, how to research a topic, and how to make my case or present my point of view more effectively. But the more I learn, the more I value the truths of salvation, those simple but profound verities that soothe and settle and sanctify human hearts. I appreciate knowing that the order of the cosmos points toward a Providential Hand; I am deeply grateful to know, by the power of the Holy Ghost, that there is a God and that he is our Father in heaven. I appreciate knowing something about the social, political, and religious world into which Jesus of Nazareth was born; I am deeply grateful for the witness of the Spirit that he is indeed God's Almighty Son. I appreciate knowing something about the social and intellectual climate of nineteenth-century America; I am grateful to have, burning within my soul, a testimony that the Father and the Son appeared to Joseph Smith in the Spring of 1820, and that The Church of Jesus Christ of Latter-day Saints is truly the kingdom of God on earth. In short, the more I encounter men's approximations to the truth, the more I treasure those absolute truths that make known "things as they really are, and . . . things as they really will be" (Jacob 4:13; compare D&C 93:24). In fact, the more we learn, the more we begin to realize what we do not know, the more we feel the need to consider ourselves "fools before God" (2 Nephi 9:42).

Those who choose to follow the Brethren, believe in and

teach the scriptures, and be loyal to the Church—no matter the extent of their academic training or intellectual capacity—open themselves to ridicule from the cynic and the critic. "True religion deals with spiritual things," Elder Bruce R. McConkie testified. "We do not come to a knowledge of God and his laws through intellectuality, or by research, or by reason. . . . In their sphere, education and intellectuality are devoutly to be desired.

"But when contrasted with spiritual endowments, they are of but slight and passing worth. From an eternal perspective what each of us needs is a Ph.D. in faith and righteousness. The things that will profit us everlastingly are not the power to reason, but the ability to receive revelation; not the truths learned by study, but the knowledge gained by faith; not what we know about the things of the world, but our knowledge of God and his laws."[11]

Ultimately, doctrinal truth comes not through the explorations of scholars but through the revelations of God to apostles and prophets. And if such a position be labeled as narrow, parochial, or anti-intellectual, then so be it. I cast my lot with the prophets.

CHAPTER 3

WHAT IS OUR DOCTRINE?

We have been charged to "teach one another the doctrine of the kingdom. Teach ye diligently," the Lord implores, "and my grace shall attend you, that you may be instructed more perfectly in theory, in principle, in doctrine, in the law of the gospel, in all things that pertain unto the kingdom of God, that are expedient for you to understand" (D&C 88:77–78).

But what exactly are we to teach? What is doctrine? Let me affirm that the right and authority to declare, interpret, and clarify doctrine rests exclusively with living apostles and prophets. I thus speak only *about* doctrine and in no way attempt to reach beyond my own stewardship as a professor of religion at Brigham Young University.

DOCTRINE: ITS PURPOSE, POWER, AND PURITY

Doctrine is "the basic body of Christian teaching or understanding (2 Timothy 3:16). Christian doctrine is composed of teachings which are to be handed on through instruction and proclamation. . . . Religious doctrine deals with the ultimate and most comprehensive questions."[1] Further, "gospel doctrine is synonymous with the truths of salvation. It comprises the tenets, teachings, and true theories found in the scriptures; it includes the principles, precepts, and revealed philosophies of pure religion;

prophetic dogmas, maxims, and views are embraced within its folds; the Articles of Faith are part and portion of it, as is every inspired utterance of the Lord's agents."[2]

The central, saving doctrine is that Jesus is the Christ, the Son of God, the Savior and Redeemer of humankind; that he lived, taught, healed, suffered and died for our sins; and that he rose from the dead the third day with a glorious, immortal, resurrected body (1 Corinthians 15:1–4; D&C 76:40–42). The Prophet Joseph Smith spoke of these central truths as the "fundamental principles" of our religion, to which all other doctrines are but appendages.[3]

Elder Boyd K. Packer taught: "Truth, glorious truth, proclaims there is . . . a Mediator. . . . Through Him mercy can be fully extended to each of us without offending the eternal law of justice. *This truth is the very root of Christian doctrine.* You may know much about the gospel as it branches out from there, but if you only know the branches and those branches do not touch that root, if they have been cut free from that truth, there will be no life nor substance nor redemption in them."[4]

Such counsel points us toward that which is of most worth in sermons and in the classroom, that which should receive our greatest emphasis. There is power in doctrine, power in the word (Alma 31:5), power to heal the wounded soul (Jacob 2:8), power to transform human behavior. "True doctrine, understood, changes attitudes and behavior," Elder Packer explained. "The study of the doctrines of the gospel will improve behavior quicker than a study of behavior will improve behavior. . . . That is why we stress so forcefully the study of the doctrines of the gospel."[5] Elder Neal A. Maxwell also pointed out that "doctrines believed and practiced do change and improve us, while insuring our vital access to the Spirit. Both outcomes are crucial."[6]

We are under obligation to learn the doctrines, teach them

properly, and bind ourselves to speak and act in harmony with them. Only in this way can we perpetuate truth in a world filled with error, avoid deception, focus on what matters most, and find joy and happiness in the process. "I have spoken before," President Gordon B. Hinckley stated, "about the importance of keeping the doctrine of the Church pure, and seeing that it is taught in all of our meetings. I worry about this. Small aberrations in doctrinal teaching can lead to large and evil falsehoods."[7]

How do we keep the doctrine pure? What might we do?

1. We can teach directly from the scriptures, the standard works. The scriptures contain the mind and will and voice and word of the Lord (D&C 68:3–4) to men and women in earlier days and thus teach doctrine and applications that are both timely and timeless. "All scripture given by inspiration of God, is profitable for doctrine, for reproof, for correction, for instruction in righteousness; that the man [or woman] of God may be perfect, thoroughly furnished unto all good works" (Joseph Smith Translation, 2 Timothy 3:16–17).

2. We can present the doctrine in the same way the prophets in our own day present it (D&C 52:9, 36), both in content and in emphasis. Mormon wrote: "Alma, having authority from God, ordained priests; . . . and he commanded them that *they should teach nothing save it were the things which he had taught*" (Mosiah 18:18–19; emphasis added). "Therefore they did assemble themselves together in different bodies, being called churches; every church having their priests and their teachers, and *every priest preaching the word according as it was delivered to him by the mouth of Alma*. And thus, notwithstanding there being many churches they were all one church, yea, even the church of God" (Mosiah 25:21–22; emphasis added).

3. We can pay special attention to scriptural commentary offered by living apostles and prophets in general conference,

cross-reference that commentary into our scriptures, and teach this commentary with the scriptures. We can study, for example, what has been taught in recent general conferences:

- President Gordon B. Hinckley taught in October 2003 about coming unto Christ.
- Elder Jeffrey R. Holland taught in April 2002 about the parable of the prodigal son.
- Elder M. Russell Ballard taught in October 2001 about "Who is my neighbor?" and the "doctrine of inclusion."
- Elder Joseph B. Wirthlin taught in April 2001 about the principles of fasting.
- Elder Robert D. Hales taught in October 2000 about the covenant of baptism.
- Elder Dallin H. Oaks taught in October 2000 about conversion and the parable of the workers in the vineyard. And so forth.

4. We can teach the gospel with plainness and simplicity, focus on fundamentals, and emphasize what matters most. We do not tell all we know, nor do we teach on the edge of our knowledge. The Prophet Joseph Smith explained that "it is not always wise to relate all the truth. Even Jesus, the Son of God, had to refrain from doing so, and had to restrain His feelings many times for the safety of Himself and His followers, and had to conceal the righteous purposes of His heart in relation to many things pertaining to His Father's kingdom."[8]

5. We can acknowledge that some things we simply do not know. President Joseph F. Smith declared: "It is no discredit to our intelligence or to our integrity to say frankly in the face of a hundred speculative questions, 'I do not know.'

"One thing is certain, and that is, God has revealed enough to our understanding for our exaltation and for our happiness.

Let the Saints, then, utilize what they already have; be simple and unaffected in their religion, both in thought and word, and they will not easily lose their bearings and be subjected to the vain philosophies of man."[9]

DOCTRINAL PARAMETERS

In recent years, I have tried to look beneath the surface to discern the nature of the objections that so many in the religious world have toward us as Latter-day Saints. To be sure, the phenomenal growth of the Church poses a real threat to many; more specifically, Christian groups resent the way we "steal their sheep." We are not in the line of historic Christianity and thus are neither Catholic nor Protestant. We believe in scripture beyond the Bible and in continuing revelation through apostles and prophets. We do not accept the concepts of God, Christ, and the Godhead that grew out of the post–New Testament church councils. All of these things constitute reasons why many Protestants and Catholics label us as non-Christian. We have tried, with some success, I think, to speak of ourselves as "Christian but different." There is another reason we as Latter-day Saints are suspect, however, a reason that underlies and buttresses large amounts of anti-Mormon propaganda, namely, what they perceive to be some of our "unusual doctrines," many of which were presented by a few Church leaders of the past.

Let me illustrate with an experience I had recently. A Baptist minister and I were chatting in my office about a number of things, including doctrine. He said, "Bob, you people believe in such strange things!"

"Like what?" I asked.

"Oh, for example," he said, "you believe in blood atonement. And that affects Utah's insistence on retaining death by a firing squad."

I responded, "No, we don't."

"Yes, you do," he came right back. "I know of several statements by Brigham Young, Heber C. Kimball, and Jedediah Grant that teach such things."

"I'm aware of those statements," I said. I then found myself saying something I had never voiced before: "Yes, they were taught, but *they do not represent the doctrine of our Church*. We believe in the blood atonement of Jesus Christ, and that alone."

My friend didn't miss a beat: "What do you mean those statements don't represent the doctrine of your church? They were spoken by major Church leaders."

I explained that such statements were made, for the most part, during the so-called Mormon Reformation and they were examples of a kind of revival rhetoric through which Church leaders were striving to "raise the bar" for members' obedience and faithfulness. I assured him that the Church, by its own canonical standards, does not have the right or the power to take a person's life because of disobedience or even apostasy (D&C 134:10). I read to him a passage from the Book of Mormon in which the Nephite prophets had resorted to "exceeding harshness, . . . continually reminding [the people] of death, and the duration of eternity, and the judgments and the power of God, . . . and exceedingly great plainness of speech" in order to "keep them from going down speedily to destruction" (Enos 1:23).

My answer seemed to satisfy him to some extent, but then he said, "Bob, many of my fellow Christians have commented that is hard to figure out what Mormons believe. They say it's like trying to nail green Jell-O to the wall! What *do* you people believe? How do you decide what *is* your doctrine and what is not?"

I recognized that we were in the midst of a very important conversation, one that was pushing me to the limit and requiring that I do some deep thinking. His questions were valid. They were in no way mean-spirited. They were not intended to entrap or embarrass me or the Church. He simply was seeking information.

I said, "You've asked some excellent questions. Let me see what I can do to answer them." Then I suggested that he consider the following three ideas:

1. The teachings of the Church today have a rather narrow focus, range, and direction; central and saving doctrine is what we are called upon to teach and emphasize, not tangential and peripheral teachings.

2. Very often what is drawn from Church leaders of the past is, like the matter of blood atonement, either misquoted, misrepresented, or taken out of context. Further, not everything that was ever spoken or written by a Church leader in the past is a part of what we teach today. Ours is a living, dynamic Church, a living tree of life (D&C 1:30). We are commanded to heed the words of living oracles (D&C 90:3–5).

3. In determining whether something is a part of the doctrine of the Church, we might ask: Is it found within the four standard works? Within official declarations or proclamations? Is it taught or discussed in general conference or other official gatherings by general Church leaders today? Is it found in the general handbooks or approved curriculum of the Church today? If it meets at least one of these criteria, we can appropriately teach it. We might also add that within the category of "all that God does reveal" (Article of Faith 9) would be certain matters about which we are enjoined to maintain a sacred silence. The content of the temple endowment today, for example, would certainly be considered a part of the doctrine of the Church.

A significant proportion of anti-Mormon writing focuses on statements by Church leaders of the past that deal with peripheral issues. No one criticizes us for believing in God, the divinity of Jesus Christ or his atoning work, the literal bodily resurrection of the Savior and the eventual resurrection of mankind, baptism by immersion, the gift of the Holy Ghost, the sacrament of the Lord's Supper, and so forth. But we are challenged regularly for statements in our literature on such matters as—

- God's life before he was God;
- how Jesus was conceived;
- the specific fate of sons of perdition;
- teachings about Adam as God;
- details of what it means to become like God hereafter;
- whether plural marriage is essential to one's exaltation;
- why blacks were denied the priesthood before 1978, and so forth.

We must never allow someone not of our faith to instruct us on what we as Latter-day Saints believe. If an active, practicing member of The Church of Jesus Christ of Latter-day Saints does not have the right to introduce or declare doctrine, why should someone from outside the faith be allowed to do so?

Loyalty to Men Called as Prophets

We love the scriptures and thank God regularly for them. We also believe that we can have confidence in and even reverence for holy writ without believing that every word between Genesis 1:1 and Revelation 22:21 is the word-for-word dictation of the Almighty or that the Bible now reads as it has always read. Indeed, our own latter-day scriptures attest that plain and precious truths and many covenants of the Lord were taken away or kept back from the Bible before it was compiled (1 Nephi 13:20–29; Moses 1:40–41; Article of Faith 8).[10] But we still cherish the sacred volume, recognize and teach the doctrines of salvation within it, and seek to pattern our lives according to its timeless teachings.

In like manner, we can sustain with all our hearts the prophets and apostles without believing that they are perfect or that everything they say or do is exactly what God wants said and done. In short, we do not believe in apostolic or prophetic infallibility. Moses made mistakes, but we love and sustain him and accept his writings nonetheless. Peter made mistakes, but we still honor him and study his words. Paul made mistakes, but we admire his boldness and dedication and treasure his epistles. James pointed out that Elijah "was a man subject to like passions as we are" (James 5:17), and the Prophet Joseph Smith taught that "a prophet [is] a prophet only when he [is] acting as such."[11]

On another occasion the Prophet declared: "I told them I was but a man, and they must not expect me to be perfect; if they expected perfection from me, I should expect it from them; but if they would bear with my infirmities and the infirmities of the brethren, I would likewise bear with their infirmities."[12] "I can fellowship the President of the Church," said Lorenzo Snow, "if he does not know everything I know. . . . I saw the . . . imperfections in [Joseph Smith]. . . . I thanked God that He would put upon a man who had those imperfections the power and authority he placed upon him . . . for I knew that I myself had weakness, and I thought there was a chance for me."[13]

Every member of the Church, including those called to guide its destiny, has the right to be wrong at one time or another—to say something that simply isn't true. They also have the right to improve their views, to change their minds and correct mistakes as new light and new truth become available. The Prophet Joseph once remarked: "I did not like the old man [Brother Pelatiah Brown] being called up for erring in doctrine. . . . It does not prove that a man is not a good man because he errs in doctrine."[14] Elder Bruce R. McConkie stated that he did "not get very troubled about an honest and a sincere person who makes a mistake in doctrine, provided that it is a mistake of the intellect or a mistake of understanding, and provided it is not on a great basic and fundamental principle." He also explained that "if you err in some doctrines, and I have, and all of us have, what we want to do is get the further light and knowledge that we ought to receive and get our souls in tune and clarify our thinking."[15]

As we have been reminded again and again, whom God calls, God qualifies. God calls his prophets. He empowers and strengthens the individual, provides an eternal perspective, loosens his tongue, and enables him to make known divine truth. But being called as an apostle or even as president of the Church does not remove the man from mortality or make him perfect. Elder David O. McKay explained that "when God makes the prophet He does not unmake the man."[16]

"I was this morning introduced to a man from the east," Joseph Smith stated. "After hearing my name, he remarked that I was nothing but a man, indicating by this expression, that he had supposed that a person to whom the Lord should see fit to reveal His will, must be something more than a man. He seemed to have forgotten the saying that fell from the lips of St. James, that Elias [Elijah] was a man subject to like passions as we are, yet he had such power with God, that He, in answer to his prayers, shut the heavens that they gave no rain for the space of three years and six months."[17]

"With all their inspiration and greatness," Elder Bruce R. McConkie declared, "prophets are yet mortal men with imperfections common to mankind in general. They have their opinions and prejudices and are left to work out their own problems without inspiration in many instances."[18] "Thus the opinions and views, even of a prophet, may contain error, unless those opinions and views were inspired by the Spirit."[19]

"There have been times," Elder Harold B. Lee pointed out, "when even the President of the Church has not been moved upon by the Holy Ghost. There is, I suppose you'd say, a classic story of Brigham Young in the time when Johnston's army was on the move. The Saints were all inflamed, and President Young had his feelings whetted to fighting pitch. He stood up in the morning session of general conference and preached a sermon vibrant with defiance at the approaching army, declaring an intention to oppose them and drive them back. In the afternoon he rose and said that Brigham Young had been talking in the morning but the Lord was going to talk now. He then delivered an address the tempo of which was the exact opposite of the morning sermon.

"Whether that happened or not, it illustrates a principle: that the Lord can move upon His people but they may speak on occasions their own opinions."[20]

In 1865 the First Presidency counseled the Latter-day Saints: "We do not wish incorrect and unsound doctrines to be handed down to posterity under the sanction of great names, to be received and valued by future generations as authentic and reliable, creating labor and difficulties for our successors to perform and contend with, which we ought not to transmit to them. The interests of posterity are, to a certain extent, in our hands. Errors in history and in doctrine, if left uncorrected by us who are conversant with the events, and who are in a position to judge of the truth or falsity of the doctrines, would go to our children as though we had sanctioned and endorsed them. . . . We know what sanctity there is always attached to the writings of men who have passed away, especially to the writings of Apostles, when none of their contemporaries are left, and we, therefore, feel the necessity of being watchful upon these points."[21]

President Gordon B. Hinckley stated: "I have worked with seven Presidents of this Church. I have recognized that all have been human. But I have never been concerned over this. They may have had some weaknesses. But this has never troubled me. I know that the God of heaven has used mortal men throughout history to accomplish His divine purposes."[22] President Hinckley pleaded with the Saints that "as we continue our search for truth . . . we look for strength and goodness rather than weakness and foibles in those who did so great a work in their time.

"We recognize that our forebears were human. They doubtless made mistakes. . . .

"There was only one perfect man who ever walked the earth. The Lord has used imperfect people in the process of building his perfect society. If some of them occasionally stumbled, or if their characters may have been slightly flawed in one way or another, the wonder is the greater that they accomplished so much."[23]

Prophets are men called of God to serve as covenant spokesmen for his children on earth, and thus we should never take lightly what they say. The early Brethren of this dispensation were the living prophets for their contemporaries, and much of what we believe and practice today rests upon the doctrinal foundation they laid. But the work of the Restoration entails a gradual unfolding of divine truth in a line-upon-line fashion. Some years ago my friend and colleague Joseph McConkie remarked to a group of religious educators: "We have the scholarship of the early brethren to build upon; we have the advantage of additional history; we have inched our way up the mountain of our destiny and now stand in a position to see things with greater clarity than did they. . . . We live in finer houses than did our pioneer forefathers, but this does not argue that we are better or that our rewards will be greater. In like manner our understanding of gospel principles should be better housed, and we should constantly be seeking to make it so. There is no honor in our reading by oil lamps when we have been granted better light."[24]

Ultimately the Lord will hold us responsible for the extent to which we give heed to the teachings, direction, and focus provided by the living oracles of our own day. Their teaching, direction, and focus come to us by means of their commentary upon canonized scripture as well as the living scripture that is delivered through them by the power of the Holy Ghost (D&C 68:3–4).

FACING HARD ISSUES

My experience suggests that anti-Mormon activities will probably continue to increase in volume, at least until the Savior returns and shuts down the presses. Because we believe in a falling away and the consequent need for a restoration of the fulness of the gospel, we will never be fully accepted by those who claim to have all the truth they need in the Bible. But let us note two things about anti-Mormonism.

First, anti-Mormon material affects more than those who are not Latter-day Saints. Not only does it sometimes deter or frighten investigators but it also troubles far more members of the Church than I had previously realized. I receive at least ten phone calls, letters, or emails per week from members throughout the Church asking challenging questions that have been raised by their neighbors or by some propaganda they have read. A short time ago a young man (married, with a family) phoned me in the late afternoon, apologized for the interruption, and told me that he was teetering on the edge of leaving the Church because of his doubts. He asked several questions; I responded to each one and bore my testimony. After about half an hour, he offered profound thanks, saying that he felt he would be okay now. Such an experience is not uncommon. Materials antagonistic to Latter-day Saints and our beliefs are here to stay, and they affect adversely both Latter-day Saints and those of other faiths.

Second, critics of the Church often use our own materials against us. They don't need to create new material; they simply dig up and repackage what some of our leaders have said in the past that today would not be considered part of the doctrine of the Church. As Latter-day Saints, being eager to sustain and uphold our leaders, we hesitate to suggest that something taught by President Brigham Young or Elders Orson Pratt or Orson Hyde might not be in harmony with unfolding truth as God has made it known to us "line upon line, precept upon precept" since their time (Isaiah 28:10; 2 Nephi 28:30).

Not long ago a colleague and I were in southern California speaking to a group of about five hundred people, both Latter-day Saint and Protestant. During the question-and-answer phase of the program, someone asked the inevitable: "Are you really Christian? Do you, as many claim, worship a different Jesus?"

I answered that we worship the Christ of the New Testament, that we believe wholeheartedly in his virgin birth, his divine Sonship, his miracles, his transforming teachings, his atoning sacrifice, and his bodily resurrection from the dead. I added that we also believe in the teachings of and about Christ found in the Book of Mormon and modern revelation. After the meeting an LDS woman came up to me and said: "You didn't tell the truth about what we believe!"

Startled, I asked, "What do you mean?"

She responded, "You said we believe in the virgin birth of Christ, and you know very well we don't believe that."

"Yes, we do," I retorted.

She then said with a great deal of emotion, "I want to believe you, but people have told me for years that we believe that God the Father had sexual relations with Mary and thereby Jesus was conceived."

I looked her in the eye and said, "I'm aware of that teaching, but that is not the doctrine of the Church—that is not what we teach in the Church today. Have you ever heard the Brethren teach it in general conference? Is it in the standard works, the curricular materials, or the handbooks of the Church? Is it a part of an official declaration or proclamation?"

A five-hundred-pound weight seemed to come off her shoulders. Tears welled up in her eyes, and she said simply, "Thank you, Brother Millet."

Some time ago, Pastor Greg Johnson and I met with an Evangelical Christian congregation just outside Salt Lake City. The minister had invited us to make a presentation ("An Evangelical and a Latter-day Saint in Dialogue") that we had made several times before in different parts of the country. The purpose of our presentation is to model the kind of relationships people with differing religious views can have. This presentation has proven, in my estimation, to be a most effective bridge-building exercise.

On that particular night, the first question asked by someone in the audience was on DNA and the Book of Mormon. I commented briefly and indicated that a more detailed (and informed) response would be forthcoming soon in a journal article by a biologist at Brigham Young University. Many, many hands flew into the air. I called on a woman close to the front of the church. She asked, "How do you deal with the Adam-God doctrine?"

I answered, "Thank you for that question. It gives me an opportunity to explain a principle early in our exchange that will lay the foundation for other things to be said." I then briefly addressed the questions "What is our doctrine? What do we teach today?" I indicated if some teaching or idea was not in the standard works, not among official declarations or proclamations, was not taught currently by living apostles or prophets in general conference or other official gatherings, or was not in the general handbooks or official curriculum of the Church, it was probably *not* a part of the doctrine or teachings of the Church.

I was surprised when my pastor friend then said to the group: "Are you listening? Do you hear what Bob is saying? This is important! It's time for us to stop criticizing Latter-day Saints on matters they don't even teach today."

Two things happened immediately. First, the hands of many questioners went down. Second, the tone of the meeting changed quite dramatically. The questions asked thereafter were not baiting or challenging but rather efforts to clarify understanding. For example, the last question was asked by a middle-aged man, who stood up and said, "I for one would like to thank you, from the bottom of my heart, for what you have done here tonight. This thrills my soul. I think this is what Jesus would do. I have lived in Utah for many years, and I have many LDS friends. We get along okay; we don't fight and quarrel over religious matters. But we really don't talk with one another about the things that matter most to us, that is, our faith. I don't plan to become a Latter-day Saint, and I'm certain my Mormon friends don't plan to become Evangelical, but I would like to find more effective ways to talk heart to heart. Could you two make a few suggestions on how we can deepen and sweeten our relationships with our LDS neighbors?"

These experiences highlighted for me the challenge we face. I have no hesitation telling an individual or a group "I don't know" when I am asked why men are ordained to the priesthood and women are not, why blacks were denied the blessings of the priesthood for almost a century and a half, and several other matters that have neither been revealed nor clarified by those holding the proper keys. The difficulty comes when someone in the past *has* spoken on these matters and *has* put forward ideas that are out of harmony with what we teach today, especially when those teachings are still available, either in print or among the everyday conversations of Church members, and have never been corrected or clarified. The questions underlying this difficulty are simply, "What is our doctrine? What are the teachings of the Church today?" If the Saints—and the larger religious world—knew the answer to those questions, that understanding would no doubt enhance our missionary effort, our convert retention, our activation efforts, and the image and overall strength of the Church. If presented properly, such an approach to understanding doctrine does not weaken faith or create doubts. It could do much to focus the Saints more fully on the central, saving verities of the gospel.

Inevitably some, whether Church members or persons of other faiths, who are told that everything said by a Latter-day Saint prophet or apostle may not be a part of the doctrine of the Church or what we teach today will ask: "Well then, what *else* did this Church leader teach that is not considered doctrine today? How can we confidently accept anything else he taught? What other directions taken or procedures pursued by the Church in an earlier time do we not follow in our day?" The truth is, for Latter-day Saints, that response is like throwing the baby out with the bath water. We must never allow ourselves to overgeneralize and thus overreact. Nor must we be guilty of discounting all that is good and uplifting and divinely given because of an aberration. After all, just because a prophet once expressed an opinion or perhaps put forward a doctrinal view that needed further clarification or even correction does not invalidate all else that he did or said. I would certainly hate to be judged that way, and I have no desire to be guilty of judging the Lord's anointed by that standard. God calls his prophets, and God corrects them. He knows their strengths, and he knows their weakness. He teaches them, as he teaches us, "line upon line, precept upon precept" (D&C 98:12).

Those of other faiths who criticize the Church and question its truthfulness because of past teachings from Church leaders that are not accepted as doctrine today would do well to ask themselves if they are prepared to apply the same standards of judgment to their own tradition, their own prominent speakers, or their own past. That is like asking someone, "Would you like to better understand Roman Catholicism today? Then study carefully the atrocities of the Crusades or the horrors of the Inquisition." Or, "Would you like a deeper glimpse into the hearts of Lutherans today? Then study the anti-Semitic writings of Martin Luther." Or, "Would you like to better understand Southern Baptists? Then read the many sermons of Baptist preachers during the time of the Civil War who used biblical passages to justify the practice of slavery." When individuals emphasize moments in Latter-day Saint history of which we're not particularly proud or cite statements that do not today represent the doctrine of the Church, it is well to remember that these moments or statements are anomalies. They are unusual, atypical examples of Latter-day Saint teachings or practices. It is unfortunately true that such anomalies can be identified in other religious traditions as well.

True doctrine has what might be called "sticking power"—it is taught and discussed and perpetuated over time, and with the passing of years seems to take on greater significance. Time, experience, careful thought, and subsequent revelation through prophets—these all either reinforce and support a particular idea or bring it into question and eventually discount it. To the Latter-day Saints the Lord Jesus declared: "And I give unto you a commandment, that ye shall forsake all evil and cleave unto all good, that ye shall live by every word which proceedeth forth out of the mouth of God. For he will give unto the faithful line upon line, precept upon precept; and I will try you and prove you herewith." (D&C 98:11–12; compare Isaiah 28:9–10; 2 Nephi 28:30).

In the early days of the restored Church, for example, an idea was perpetuated by some that sons of perdition would eventually be restored and allowed to experience mortality again. Not only did Joseph Smith denounce the idea but modern revelation that speaks of the inseparable union of body and spirit in the resurrection defies it.[25] On the other hand, doctrines such as the proper relationship between the grace of God and the good works of man, the redemption of the dead, exaltation through eternal marriage, and the overall significance of temples—these matters have been discussed and clarified and reinforced by those holding the keys of the kingdom to such extent that we not only accept them fully as true and from God but we also grasp their profundity even more than when they were first made known. Falsehood and error will eventually be detected and dismissed by those charged to guide the destiny of the kingdom of God. Truth, as Joseph Smith observed, "will cut its own way."[26]

WHERE IS SAFETY?

One way to keep our doctrine pure is to present the gospel message the way the prophets and apostles today present it. Similarly, our explanations of hard doctrines, or deeper doctrines, should not go beyond what the prophets teach today.

My first illustration of this approach is an extremely sensitive matter that continues to affect the number and commitment of converts in the Church. I speak of the matter of blacks and the priesthood. Like many other Latter-day Saints, I was raised in the Church and was well aware of the priesthood restriction. For as long as I can remember, the explanation for why our black brethren and sisters were denied the full blessings of the priesthood (including the temple) was some variation on the theme that they had been less valiant in the premortal life and thus had come to earth under a curse, an explanation that has been perpetuated as doctrine for most of our Church's history. As a child I had committed to memory the article of our faith that states that men and women will be punished for their own sins and not for Adam's transgression (Article of Faith 2) and later read that "the sins of the parents cannot be answered upon the heads of the children" (Moses 6:54), but I had assumed those principles somehow did not apply to blacks.

In June 1978 everything changed—not just who could be ordained to the priesthood but also the explanation for why the restriction had been in place at all. Elder Dallin H. Oaks was asked: "As much as any doctrine the Church has espoused, or controversy the Church has been embroiled in, this one [the priesthood restriction] seems to stand out. Church members seemed to have less to go on to get a grasp of the issue. Can you address why this was the case, and what can be learned from it?"

Elder Oaks answered: "If you read the scriptures with this question in mind, 'Why did the Lord command this or why did he command that,' you find that in less than one in a hundred commands was any reason given. It's not the pattern of the Lord to give reasons. We can put reason to revelation. We can put reasons to commandments. When we do we're on our own. Some people put reasons to the one we're talking about here, and they turned out to be spectacularly wrong. There is a lesson in that. The lesson I've drawn from that [is that] I decided a long time ago that I had faith in the command and I had no faith in the reasons that had been suggested for it."

Then came the follow-up question: "Are you referring to reasons given even by general authorities?"

Elder Oaks responded: "Sure. I'm referring to reasons given by general authorities and reasons elaborated upon that reason by others. The whole set of reasons seemed to me to be unnecessary risk-taking. . . . Let's don't make the mistake that's been made in the past, here and in other areas, trying to put reasons to revelation. The reasons turn out to be man-made to a great extent. The revelations are what we sustain as the will of the Lord and that's where safety lies."[27]

In other words, we really do not know why the restriction on the priesthood existed. "I don't know" is the correct answer when we are asked why. The priesthood was restricted "for reasons which we believe are known to God, but which he has not made fully known to man."[28] Elder Bruce R. McConkie taught this principle in his August 1978 address to the Church Educational System: "Forget everything that I have said, or what President Brigham Young or President George Q. Cannon or whosoever has said in days past that is contrary to the present revelation. We spoke with a limited understanding and without the light and knowledge that now has come into the world.

"We get our truth and our light line upon line and precept upon precept. We have now had added a new flood of intelligence and light on this particular subject, and it erases all the darkness and all the views and all the thoughts of the past. They don't matter any more. . . .

"It is a new day and a new arrangement, and the Lord has now given the revelation that sheds light out into the world on this subject. As to any slivers of light or any particles of darkness of the past, we forget about them."[29]

It seems to me, therefore, that we as Latter-day Saints have two problems to solve in making the restored gospel available more extensively to people of color. First, we need to have our hearts and minds purified of all pride and all prejudice. Second, we need to dismiss all explanations for the restriction and indicate that though we simply do not know why the restriction existed, the blessings of the restored gospel are now fully available to all who prepare themselves to receive them. Elder M. Russell Ballard observed that "we don't know all of the reasons why the Lord does what He does. We need to be content that someday we'll fully understand it."[30]

My second illustration of why I think we should present the gospel message the way prophets and apostles present it today is of a somewhat different order. I have rarely addressed questions from a group of persons not of our faith that have not included inquiries about our doctrine of God and the Godhead, particularly the teachings of Joseph Smith and Lorenzo Snow. I generally do not have much difficulty explaining our view of how through the Atonement man can eventually become like God and become more and more Christlike. For that matter, orthodox Christianity, a huge segment of the Christian world, still holds to a view of theosis, or human deification. The Bible itself teaches that men and women may become "partakers of the divine nature" (2 Peter 1:4), "joint-heirs with Christ" (Romans 8:17), gain "the mind of Christ" (1 Corinthians 2:16), and become perfect, even as our Father in heaven is perfect (Matthew 5:48). The apostle John declared: "Beloved, now are we the [children] of God, and it doth not yet appear what we shall be: but we know that, when he shall appear, we shall be like him; for we shall see him as he is" (1 John 3:2). Perhaps more important, this doctrine is taught powerfully in modern revelation (D&C 76:58; 132:19–20).

The tougher issue for many Christians is the accompanying doctrine set forth in the King Follett Sermon[31] and the Lorenzo Snow couplet[32]—namely, that God was once a man. Latter-day scriptures state unequivocally that God is a man, a Man of Holiness (Moses 6:57), who possesses a body of flesh and bones (D&C 130:22). These concepts are clearly a part of the doctrinal restoration. We teach that man is not of a lower order or a different species from God. This, of course, makes many of our Christian friends extremely nervous (if not angry), for it appears to them that we are lowering God in the scheme of things and thus attempting to bridge the Creator-creature chasm.

About all we can say in response to questions about our doctrine of God and the Godhead is that we know what we know as a result of modern revelation and that from our perspective the distance between God and man is overwhelming, almost infinite. Our Father in heaven is indeed omnipotent, omniscient, and, by the power of his Holy Spirit, omnipresent. He is a glorified, exalted, resurrected being, "the only supreme governor and independent being in whom all fullness and perfection dwell; . . . in him every good gift and every good principle dwell; . . . he is the Father of lights; in him the principle of faith dwells independently, and he is the object in whom the faith of all other rational and accountable beings center for life and salvation."[33] Modern revelation attests that the Almighty sits enthroned "with glory, honor, power, majesty, might, dominion, truth, justice, judgment, mercy, and an infinity of fulness" (D&C 109:77).

What do we know beyond the truth that God is an exalted Man? What do we know of his mortal existence? What do we know of the time before he became God? Nothing. We really do not know more than what the Prophet Joseph Smith stated, and that is precious little. Insights concerning God's life before Godhood are not found in the standard works, in official declarations or proclamations, or in current handbooks or curricular materials, nor are doctrinal expositions on the subject delivered in general conference today. This topic is not what we would call a central and saving doctrine, one that we must believe (or understand) to hold a temple recommend or be in good standing in the Church.

This latter illustration highlights an important point: *Doctrine* means "teaching." If the general authorities do not teach something today, it is not part of our doctrine today. That does not, however, mean that a particular teaching is necessarily untrue. A teaching may be true and yet not be a part of what is taught and emphasized in the Church today. In fact, if the Brethren do not teach it today, if it is not taught directly in the standard works, or if it is not found in our correlated curriculum, whether it is true or not may actually be irrelevant.

It would be well for us to apply a lesson from President Harold B. Lee: "With respect to doctrines and meanings of scriptures, let me give you a safe counsel. It is usually not well to use a single passage of scripture [or, I would add, a single sermon] in proof of a point of doctrine unless it is confirmed by modern revelation or by the Book of Mormon. . . . To single out a passage of scripture to prove a point, unless it is [so] confirmed . . . is always a hazardous thing."[34]

CONCLUSION

In a very real sense, we as Latter-day Saints are spoiled. We have been given so much knowledge from on high relative to the nature of God, Christ, man, the plan of salvation, and the overall purpose of life here and the glory to be had hereafter that we are inclined to expect to have all the answers to all the questions of life. Elder Neal A. Maxwell pointed out that "the exhilarations of discipleship exceed its burdens. Hence, while journeying through our Sinai, we are nourished in the Bountiful-like oases of the Restoration. Of these oases some of our first impressions may prove to be more childish than definitive. . . . In our appreciation, little wonder some of us mistake a particular tree for the whole of an oasis, or a particularly refreshing pool for the entirety of the Restoration's gushing and living waters. Hence, in our early exclamations there may even be some unintended exaggerations. We have seen and partaken of far too much; hence, we 'cannot [speak] the smallest part [which] we feel' (Alma 26:16)."[35]

We have much, to be sure, but there are "many great and important things pertaining to the kingdom of God" yet to come forth (Article of Faith 9). The Lord stated to Joseph Smith in Nauvoo: "I deign to reveal unto my church things which have been kept hid from before the foundation of the world, things that pertain to the dispensation of the fulness of times" (D&C 124:41; compare 121:26; 128:18). As Elder Oaks observed, we have been given many commands but not all the reasons why, many of the directives but not all the explanations. It is as important for us to know *what we do not know* as it is for us to know what we know. Far too many things are taught or discussed or even argued about that belong in the realm of the unrevealed and thus the unresolved. Such matters, particularly if they do not fall within the range of revealed truth that Church leaders teach today, do not edify or inspire. Often, very often, they lead to confusion and sow discord.

That does not in any way mean that we should not seek to study and grow in our gospel understanding. Peter explained that there needs to be a reason for the hope within us (1 Peter 3:15). Our knowledge should be as settling to the mind as it is soothing to the heart. Elder Maxwell taught that some "Church members know just enough about the doctrines to converse superficially on them, but their scant knowledge about the deep doctrines is inadequate for deep discipleship (see 1 Corinthians 2:10). Thus uninformed about the deep doctrines, they make no deep change in their lives."[36]

President Hugh B. Brown once observed: "I am impressed with the testimony of a man who can stand and say he knows the gospel is true. What I would like to ask is 'But, sir, do you know the gospel?' . . . Mere testimony can be gained with but perfunctory knowledge of the Church and its teachings. . . . But to retain a testimony, to be of service in building the Lord's kingdom, requires a serious study of the gospel and knowing what it is."[37] President Brown taught that we are required only to "defend those doctrines of the church contained in the four standard works. . . . Anything beyond that by anyone is his or her own opinion and not scripture. . . . The only way I know of by which the teachings of any person or group may become binding upon the church is if the teachings have been reviewed by all the brethren, submitted to the highest councils of the church, and then approved by the whole body of the church."[38] Again, the issue is one of focus, one of emphasis—where we choose to spend our time when we teach the gospel both to Latter-day Saints and to those of other faiths.

There is a valid reason why it is difficult to tie down Latter-day Saint doctrine, one that derives from the very nature of the Restoration. That God continues to speak through his anointed servants; that He, through those servants, continues to reveal, elucidate, and clarify what has already been given; and that our canon of scripture is open, flexible, and expanding—all militate against what many in the Christian world would call a systematic theology.

It is the declaration of sound and solid doctrine, the doctrine found in scripture and taught regularly by Church leaders, that builds faith and strengthens testimony and commitment to the Lord and his kingdom. Elder Maxwell explained that "deeds *do* matter as well as doctrines, but the doctrines can move us to do the deeds, and the Spirit can help us to understand the doctrines as well as prompt us to do the deeds."[39] He also noted that "when weary legs falter and detours and roadside allurements entice, the fundamental doctrines will summon from deep within us fresh determination. Extraordinary truths can move us to extraordinary accomplishments."[40]

The teaching and application of sound doctrine are great safeguards to us in these last days, shields against the fiery darts of the adversary. Understanding true doctrine and being true to that doctrine can keep us from ignorance, from error, and from sin. The apostle Paul counseled Timothy: "If thou put the brethren [and sisters] in remembrance of these things, thou shalt be a good minister of Jesus Christ, nourished up in the words of faith and of good doctrine, whereunto thou hast attained. . . . Till I come, give attendance to reading, to exhortation, to doctrine" (1 Timothy 4:6, 13).

CHAPTER 4

WISDOM IN RESPONSE

"We are not without critics," President Gordon B. Hinckley observed, "some of whom are mean and vicious. We have always had them, and I suppose we will have them all through the future. But we shall go forward, returning good for evil, being helpful and kind and generous."[1] Thus, how we respond to criticism or how we choose to answer hard questions about our faith and way of life is important. This is especially the case as Church membership grows, as temples spread throughout the earth, and as our influence begins to be witnessed and felt more and more.

Most people who know Latter-day Saints like the way we live and even like the way we talk. They're just plain uncomfortable with some of the doctrine that underlies our behavior. In fact, our conduct and our way of life cannot be separated from our doctrine, for what we believe empowers and directs what we do. A number of years ago an article appeared in *Christianity Today* entitled "Why Your Neighbor Joined the Mormon Church." Five reasons were given:

1. The Latter-day Saints show genuine love and concern by taking care of their people.
2. They strive to build the family unit.
3. They provide for their young people.
4. Theirs is a layman's church.

5. They believe that divine revelation is the basis for their practices.

After a brief discussion of these points, the author concluded: "In a day when many are hesitant to claim that God has said anything definitive, the Mormons stand out in contrast, and many people are ready to listen to what the Mormons think the voice of God says. It is tragic that their message is false, but it is nonetheless a lesson to us that people are many times ready to hear a voice of authority."[2] In answer, we say simply that the Savior taught of the importance of judging things—prophets, for example—by their fruits, by the product of their ministry and teachings (Matthew 7:15–20). He also explained that "every plant, which my heavenly Father hath not planted, shall be rooted up" (Matthew 15:13). Evil trees cannot bring forth good fruit. Works of men eventually come to naught, but that which is of God cannot be overthrown (Acts 5:38–39; 1 John 3:7).

In encountering those who question us—whether sincere investigators or critics of the Church—certain matters are worth considering. First, each of us can have sufficient knowledge and testimony of the gospel to sustain and defend the faith; no formal schooling or training is necessary, although we may more readily provide a reason for the hope within us (1 Peter 3:15) when we have become closer acquaintances of the doctrines of the gospel. Second, although we want to be helpful where we can, we are not obligated to answer everyone's questions. In fact, some questions are best not answered at all (Alma 11:21–22). Third, as Latter-day Saints, we already know more about God and Christ and the plan of salvation than anyone who might seek to deter us from a faithful course. We need to be confident and assured in the knowledge that is ours.

Let me share some suggestions—learned through both sad

and sweet experiences—about how we might effectively deal with difficult questions posed by those not of our faith.

AVOID THE SPIRIT OF CONTENTION

Most important is to *stay in control*. Avoid the spirit of contention. There is nothing more frustrating than knowing the truth, loving the truth, sincerely desiring to share the truth, and yet being unable to communicate our deepest feelings to another person who sees things differently. Argument or disputation over sacred things causes us to forfeit the Spirit of God and thus the confirming power of our message (3 Nephi 11:28–30). We teach and we testify. Contention is unbecoming of one called to publish peace and thereby bless our brothers and sisters. In the words of Elder Marvin J. Ashton, "We have no time for contention. We only have time to be about our Father's business."[3]

In 1896 President Joseph F. Smith wrote to one of his sons who was serving as a missionary: "Kindness will beget friendship and favor, but anger or passion will drive away sympathy. To win one's respect and confidence, approach him mildly—kindly. No friendship was ever gained by an attack upon principle or upon man, but by calm reason and the lowly Spirit of truth. If you have built for a man a better house than his own, and he is willing to accept yours and forsake his, then, and not till then, should you proceed to tear down the old structure. Rotten though it may be, it will require some time for it to lose *all* its charms and fond memories of its former occupant. Therefore let *him*, not *you*, proceed to tear it away. Kindness and courtesy are the primal elements of gentility."[4]

I have been a student of the Book of Mormon for many years, and I have come to value its principles and precepts more than silver or gold. I discover new truths and new applications with new readings and new experiences in life. For example, I have read the first chapter of Alma many, many times. But in recent years a particular reading of the text brought to light a lesson, a stern warning. Speaking of events in about 90 B.C., Mormon explained: "It came to pass that whosoever did not belong to the church of God began to persecute those that did belong to the church of God, and had taken upon them the name of Christ. Yea, they did persecute them, and afflict them with all manner of words." He noted that "there was a strict law among the people of the church, that there should not any man, belonging to the church, arise and persecute those that did not belong to the church, and that there should be no persecution among themselves. Nevertheless," Mormon observed, "there were many among them"—meaning the church—"who began to be proud, and began to contend warmly with their adversaries, even unto blows; yea, they would smite one another with their fists." I have been involved in some pretty heated discussions on religious topics, but I've never been in a fist fight! Mormon pointed out that these unfortunate instances were the cause of "much affliction to the church." Why? "*For the hearts of many were hardened, and their names were blotted out,* that they were remembered no more among the people of God. And also many withdrew themselves from among them" (Alma 1:19–24; emphasis added). How tragic! Here were members of the Church of Jesus Christ whose contention for the faith cost them their faith and their Church membership.

I gained a new appreciation for that passage of scripture some years ago. I had been called to a Church writing committee and had worked closely with my colleagues for about a year. During that same time, Joseph McConkie and I had written a book on dealing responsibly with opposition to the faith. Very late one Sunday evening the phone rang. The caller introduced himself as Brother Harrison from Texas (name and location

changed). He thanked me for the book Joseph and I had written, and he said he had learned a great deal from it. I thanked
him for taking the time to call. Then he said, essentially, "Brother
Millet, as you may be aware, we have a lot of anti-Mormonism
in our area, and some of us have decided that we aren't going to
take it on the chin anymore. We're going to fight back. We have
organized a huge debate here in town between the Mormons
and the anti-Mormons. We've rented a large hall downtown and
plan to fight it out in public. I was calling to get your suggestions on how it might best be organized to accomplish the most
good."

Startled, I responded, "Do you have something to write
with?"

"Yes," he said, "go right ahead."

I began. "The first suggestion I have is . . . cancel the whole
thing."

There was a long pause. "What did you say?" he asked.

I repeated my suggestion. I could hear the emotion, the deep
frustration, in his voice when he almost shouted back: "You
don't mean that. We need to put these people in their place! My
understanding is that this is just what the Brethren want us to
do."

I replied that I had never heard one of the general Church
authorities suggest that we argue or debate about sacred things.
Rather, we teach and we testify. People are free to hear our message, weigh its relevance to their lives, consider its implications,
and ponder and pray about its truthfulness. They are free to
accept or reject or even fight against our message. But few persons join our Church because they have been argued into it. If
they do, I have serious concerns about their sticking capacity.
The caller sighed, thanked me, and hung up.

A month later, again very late on a Sunday night (nearly

midnight), he phoned again. "Brother Millet, this is Brother Harrison from Texas. Remember me? I have another question for you. What scriptures from the Bible would you suggest we use to bash our anti's and prove there are three separate Gods in the Godhead?" Again I pleaded with him to be kind and thoughtful, to teach from the scriptures of the Restoration, and bear testimony.

These phone calls continued for several months, each similar to the last, except focusing on some new doctrinal topic my friend wanted to shove down the throats of those who disagreed with him. Suddenly, I realized the calls had ceased. When I didn't hear from Brother Harrison again, I hoped that my efforts to dissuade him from his confrontational approach might have borne fruit.

Not long afterwards, the members of the writing committee I served on were talking about anti-Mormonism and some individuals who had engaged many of the issues. One colleague mentioned my Texas caller by name.

"Do you know Brother Harrison?" I asked.

"Yes, I do," he said. "Do you know him very well?"

"Only late on Sunday nights," I replied.

My colleague responded, "It's unfortunate what happened to him."

"What happened? I haven't heard anything," I said.

"Brother Harrison was excommunicated from the Church about a year ago."

I replied, "No, this can't be the same man. The person who called me was an avid defender of the faith who is trying to banish from the planet all people who reject our message."

"Yea, that's the man," my colleague said. "He became a rabid anti-anti, lost the Spirit of the Lord, and eventually lost his membership in the Church."

ANSWER THE RIGHT QUESTION

We need to listen carefully, so that we can *answer the right question*. As a young man, I had been serving a mission to the Eastern States for a grand total of two days when I was told I would be participating in a "street meeting." I didn't know what a street meeting was, but my companion assured me that it would be a most unusual experience. We met several other missionaries at the corner of Wall Street and Nassau in New York City (just across the street from the Stock Exchange), where we arranged some panel boards ("Signs of the True Church") and then set up a pulpit, literally a soapbox from which the speaker would address the public. I did indeed find the whole matter quite fascinating—until the zone leader turned to me and said, "Okay, Elder Millet. Preach the gospel."

I smiled and waited for him and the other missionaries to smile also, but they did not. "Come on, Elder," the zone leader said. "Get up on the soap box and teach the gospel."

"*Who* do you want me to teach? *What* do you want me to teach?" I asked in a rather stunned tone.

The zone leader responded, "Teach the Apostasy and the Restoration to us, to begin with, and then other people will begin to gather."

I began haltingly to say something about the falling away of the Church in the meridian of time and the loss of the priesthood through the deaths of the apostles, but one of the missionaries cried out, "Louder, Elder. Speak louder!" I raised my voice. At twelve o'clock the doors of the Stock Exchange opened, and a surprising number of people made their way over to us. Within a few moments there were probably a hundred people—all listening to me. That gave me an ounce of courage, and so I began to speak with a bit more conviction. After about ten minutes I finished and stepped down from the box. I felt good inside, like a modern-day Parley P. Pratt or Wilford Woodruff, and the missionaries began to strike up conversations with people in the crowd.

My feelings of accomplishment were interrupted by a large African-American man, who pulled me off to one side and asked whether I would answer a question or two. "Of course," I said. "I'd be more than happy to."

"Good," he said. He grabbed me by the throat and began to apply a little pressure. "I want to hold the priesthood," he declared. "My mother always wanted me to be a priest. Can you give me the priesthood?" (Remember, this was 1967, and the issue of blacks and the priesthood was an extremely sensitive matter for the Church.) The thought ran quickly through my mind: *I want to go home! How in the world did a nice boy from Louisiana get into this mess?*

After a few seconds I responded: "I'm sorry, but we cannot give you the priesthood." He increased the pressure on my throat, which, of course, restricted my breathing enough to make the situation even more uncomfortable.

"Why can't you give me the priesthood?" he demanded.

There came into my mind a thought or two, which may well have been the result more of desperation than of inspiration.

"May I ask you a few questions?" I queried.

"Sure, go ahead," he replied.

"Do you believe The Church of Jesus Christ of Latter-day Saints is the Lord's Church, the restored kingdom of God?"

"No," he said, "I don't believe God claims a certain church."

"Do you believe that God the Father and his Son Jesus Christ visited Joseph Smith in a grove of trees in upstate New York in the spring of 1820?"

"No, of course I don't believe any such thing," he said with a smirk.

"Do you believe that heavenly messengers, angels, came to Joseph Smith, laid their hands upon his head, and conferred upon him priesthood, or divine authority?"

He laughed out loud and said, "Are you kidding? I don't believe in angels."

"Then," I ventured, "I suppose we're not really denying you anything at all, are we?" He looked deep into my eyes, let go of my throat, erupted into a wide smile, patted me a couple of times on my face, and said: "That's pretty good." He walked away.

Nearly a decade passed before I fully understood what had taken place at the street meeting. It was then that I read Elder Boyd K. Packer's account of observing with much interest as President Henry D. Moyle of the First Presidency handled biting comments and baiting questions with great ease.

Elder Packer said: "'President Moyle, that was marvelous, just marvelous. How did you do it?'

"President Moyle asked, 'What do you mean?'

"I said, 'All those antagonistic questions he asked you; it was just marvelous the way you handled them. He was so antagonistic and bitter and yet the interview itself was successful.'

"I have never forgotten his answer. He said, 'I never pay any attention to the questions—that is, if the interviewer is antagonistic. If he doesn't ask the right questions, I give answers to questions he should have asked.'"[5]

If a total stranger walked up to me and asked, "Do the Mormons really believe man can become like God?" it might not be the wisest course to respond, "Yes, indeed, we do. Let me read to you the words of the Prophet Joseph Smith in his King Follett Sermon." Rather, I might begin with something like, "That's a good question. To put it into perspective, let me say that in the spring of 1820, a young boy by the name of Joseph Smith was concerned . . ."

The real issue is never the deification of man, or what God was like before he was God, or the blacks and the priesthood, or the Mountain Meadows Massacre, or plural marriage, or Adam-God. The real question facing the religious world, even though they may not realize it, is this: "Was Joseph Smith called of God?" That's the real question, the central issue, the matter to be resolved before anyone can appreciate, even in the slightest, what Mormonism is all about.

ATTEND TO GOSPEL PREREQUISITES

In talking about the gospel, we should *stay in order.* The Savior taught that gospel prerequisites should be observed when teaching sacred things (Matthew 7:6–7).[6] A person who knows very little about our doctrine, for example, will probably not understand or appreciate our teachings concerning temples, sealing powers, eternal life, or the deification of man. Joseph Smith the Prophet explained, "If we start right, it is easy to go right all the time; but if we start wrong, we may go wrong, and it [will] be a hard matter to get right."[7] It is always wise to lay a proper foundation for what is to be said. The truth can then flow more freely.

Let me illustrate. After I had been on my mission for about fifteen months, I was assigned to work in a beautiful section of Connecticut. My companion, a nice fellow to be sure, had one problem that affected the work somewhat—his mind seemed to wander much of the time.

One early summer afternoon we approached the door of a lovely small home. A woman who appeared to be about thirty-five years old opened the front door and unlatched the screen door. "Yes? Is there something I can do for you?"

It was my companion's turn to be spokesman, so Elder Jackson (not his real name) answered. "We're missionaries for The Church of Jesus Christ of Latter-day Saints. We have a message about Christ that we would like to share with you."

She looked us over very carefully. Then she responded, "I don't think so. I have my own faith."

After waiting uncomfortably for at least ten or fifteen seconds, I blurted out, "What church do you attend?"

"I didn't say I attended a church," she came right back. "I said I had my own faith."

Surprised, I asked, "Could you tell us about your faith?"

"I don't think I want to. You would make fun of me."

I assured her we would not. "What is your faith?" I asked.

"Well," she timidly declared, "I believe the physical body is the temple of God and that people ought to take better care of their bodies. For example, I think it's wrong for people to smoke or drink."

I replied that we felt her thinking was right on the mark.

She continued, "Well, there's more. I don't drink coffee or tea. What do the Mormons believe?"

It was difficult for me not to answer, but I felt I ought to allow Elder Jackson to respond to what was obviously a great teaching moment. I could almost see the wheels in his mental machinery turning. He answered, "Well, we believe in baptism for the dead."

The woman carefully pulled the screen door shut and latched it. Before closing the main door she said, with a pained look on her face, "That sounds sick."

I had some idea of what she was thinking and of how bizarre the Latter-day Saints appeared to be. Mostly I was stunned, shocked. Before we left the porch, I turned to Elder Jackson and asked in utter disbelief, "What are you doing?"

He seemed offended and asked, "We do believe in baptism for the dead, don't we?"

I said, "Yes, we do, Elder Jackson. Why didn't you tell her about polygamy?"

His response was even more stunning. "I thought about doing that next, but she closed the door."

"Elder," I said, "this lady lives the Word of Wisdom."

"I thought that was odd," he commented, as we walked to the next door.

This woman had essentially come to the door with her tin cup and said, "I thirst." We had answered, in effect, "We can fix that" and then dragged out the fire hose and drowned her in the living waters! It isn't that this woman was not bright enough to understand the concept of salvation for the dead. The problem was that we had not laid a proper doctrinal foundation. There is indeed a system of gospel prerequisites.

An account of a conversation between Peter and Clement of Rome is particularly insightful. Peter is reported to have taught: "The teaching of all doctrine has a certain order: there are some things which must be delivered first, others in the second place, and others in the third, and so on, everything in its order. *If these things be delivered in their order they become plain; but if they be brought forward out of order, they will seem to be spoken against reason.*"[8]

BE LOYAL TO THE RESTORATION

When it comes to answering questions, especially questions about distinctive LDS teachings or practices, we need to *stay in context*. We love the Bible and cherish its messages. But the Bible is not the source of our doctrine or authority, nor is much to be gained through trying to "prove" the truthfulness of the restored gospel from the Bible. Ours is an independent revelation. We know what we know about the premortal existence, priesthood, celestial marriage, baptism for the dead, the postmortal spirit world, degrees of glory, and so forth because of what God has made known through latter-day prophets, not because we are able to identify a few biblical allusions to these matters.

Some of our greatest difficulties in handling questions about our faith come when we try to establish specific doctrines of the Restoration from the Bible alone. We have an obligation—a sacred obligation—to rely upon the Book of Mormon, the Doctrine and Covenants, the Pearl of Great Price, the Joseph Smith Translation of the Bible, and especially the teachings of latter-day apostles and prophets, in establishing our doctrine. There is consummate peace and spiritual power to be derived from being loyal and true to those things the Almighty has communicated to us in our dispensation (D&C 5:10; 31:3–4; 43:15–16; 49:1–4; 84:54–61).

In September 1832 the Lord warned of a condemnation, a scourge, and a judgment, that would rest upon the whole Church until we as Latter-day Saints took seriously the Book of Mormon and the revelations of the Restoration (D&C 84:54–61). In short, loyalty should and must exist among us, loyalty to those things the Lord has given to us. We are commanded to "declare glad tidings" (Alma 39:15). And what are those tidings? Are we to go into the world and reteach the Sermon on the Mount, the Bread of Life Sermon, or any of the remarkable doctrines contained in the New Testament? We treasure the Bible and seek to safeguard its truths, but we are called upon, in the words of the Lord, to "declare the things which have been revealed to my servant, Joseph Smith, Jun." (D&C 31:4).

Elder Parley P. Pratt wrote of an incident that happened

when Joseph Smith and Sidney Rigdon were traveling in the East. "In Philadelphia, a very large church was opened for [brother Joseph] to preach in, and about three thousand people assembled to hear him. Brother Rigdon spoke first, and dwelt on the Gospel, illustrating his doctrine by the Bible. When he was through, brother Joseph arose like a lion about to roar; and being full of the Holy Ghost, spoke in great power, bearing testimony of the visions he had seen, the ministering of angels which he had enjoyed; and how he had found the plates of the Book of Mormon, and translated them by the gift and power of God. He commenced by saying: 'If nobody else had the courage to testify of so glorious a message from Heaven, and of the finding of so glorious a record, he felt to do it in justice to the people, and leave the event with God.'

"The entire congregation were astounded; electrified, as it were, and overwhelmed with the sense of the truth and power by which he spoke, and the wonders which he related. A lasting impression was made; many souls were gathered into the fold. And I bear witness, that he, by his faithful and powerful testimony, cleared his garments of their blood. Multitudes were baptized in Philadelphia and in the regions around; while, at the same time, branches were springing up in Pennsylvania, in Jersey, and in various directions."[9]

President David O. McKay related an experience that his father had while serving as a missionary in Scotland in 1880. After testifying of the call of Joseph Smith and the truths and powers associated with it but finding much opposition to these teachings, he determined "to preach just the simple principles, the atonement of the Lord Jesus Christ, the first principles of the gospel, and not bear testimony of the restoration of the gospel. . . . In a month or so he became oppressed with a gloomy, downcast feeling, and he could not enter into the spirit of his work. He did not really know what was the matter, but his mind became obstructed; his spirit became clogged; he was oppressed and hampered; and that feeling of depression continued until it weighed him down with such heaviness that he went to the Lord and said: 'Unless I can get this feeling removed, I shall have to go home. I cannot continue my work with this feeling.'

"It continued for some time after that, then, one morning, before daylight, following a sleepless night, he decided to retire to a cave near the ocean," where he could pour out his soul in prayer without interruption. He petitioned the Almighty: "'Oh, Father, what can I do to have this feeling removed? I must have it lifted or I cannot continue in this work.'" President McKay declared, "He heard a voice, as distinct as the tone I am now uttering, say: 'Testify that Joseph Smith is a Prophet of God.'" President McKay's father gained the "realization that he was there for a special mission, and that he had not given that special mission the attention which it deserved. Then he cried in his heart, 'Lord, it is enough,' and went out from the cave."[10]

While serving as the director of the institute of religion near Florida State University, I was visited several times a week by the full-time missionaries. Often their visits were accompanied with a question of some sort, usually an eagerness to get some scripture to "prove" a particular point with their investigators. More than once the elders or sisters would begin conversations with, "Brother Millet, can you give us a scripture on . . . ?" Usually, what they really wanted was a biblical passage to drive the point home.

As the months and years passed, I began to realize that I really was not helping the missionaries by supplying them with the requested biblical passages. The next time the elders dropped by, they asked me, "Brother Millet, can you give us a good scripture on eternal marriage? These people we are working with, the

Johnsons, are really sharp, but their minister told them that Jesus taught that in the resurrection there is no marrying or giving in marriage (Matthew 22:30; Luke 20:35). Did you know that?"

I told them that I was aware of the scriptural passage. Then I said, "No, elders, I can't give you a scripture on eternal marriage."

A perplexed look spread across both their faces as the senior companion asked, "You can't, or you won't?"

I answered, "I can't, and I won't." I added: "Elders, I am not aware of any specific reference to eternal marriage in the Old or the New Testament."

The senior companion went pale and stammered: "No passage in the Old or New Testament? How can that be? Don't we believe in eternal marriage?"

I replied that as far as I could remember we did in fact believe in eternal marriage. "Has it occurred to you," I continued, "that if everything we taught or believed was found in the Bible, then there would be no need for a Book of Mormon, a Doctrine and Covenants, a Pearl of Great Price, and, for that matter, a Joseph Smith and the Restoration?"

As though the missionary had come back to life, his eyes focused once again, he sat up straight, and he said, "Oh, yes, of course."

I said, "Elders, you need to sit down with the Johnsons and read together Doctrine and Covenants 132, especially verses 15 through 19. That is where eternal marriage is discussed—in modern revelation."

"But, Brother Millet," the other missionary protested, "they're not about to accept this Doctrine and Covenants stuff. They want proof from the Bible."

"Then I suppose if they're not open to the possibility of modern revelation, they're not open to Joseph Smith and thus are certainly not ready to join the Church."

My friend and colleague Joseph McConkie has written: "The message of the Restoration centers on the idea that it is not common ground we seek in sharing the gospel. There is nothing common about our message. The way we answer questions about our faith ought to be by finding the quickest and most direct route to the Sacred Grove. That is our ground. It is sacred ground. It is where the heavens are opened and the God of heaven speaks. It is where testimonies are born and the greatest truths of heaven are unveiled. It of this sacred ground that we say, *here we stand.*"[11]

CONCLUSION

President Gordon B. Hinckley declared: "If we will go forward, never losing sight of our goal, speaking ill of no one, living the great principles we know to be true, this cause will roll on in majesty and power to fill the earth. Doors now closed to the preaching of the gospel will be opened. The Almighty, if necessary, may have to shake the nations to humble them and cause them to listen to the servants of the living God. Whatever is needed will come to pass."[12]

This work is true, and because it is true, it will triumph. The destiny of the restored kingdom is set, and we need not fear for the success of the Church. The plea often repeated in scripture is "Fear not" (Daniel 10:19; Luke 12:32; Alma 7:15; D&C 68:6). The promise of Deity is encouraging and strengthening to our faith: "Verily, thus saith the Lord unto you—there is no weapon that is formed against you shall prosper; and if any man lift his voice against you he shall be confounded in mine own due time. Wherefore, keep my commandments; they are true and faithful. Even so. Amen" (D&C 71:9–11; compare 136:17). God will bring to pass his purposes; of that we can rest assured.

CHAPTER 5

THE SCRIPTURES

As The Church of Jesus Christ of Latter-day Saints continues to grow, as its influence in the world continues to be
observed and felt, more and more people will ask questions
about our faith and our way of life. Although we have neither
the time nor the energy to respond to all the questions that come
our way, especially those that are clearly intended to trap or
ensnare us, we need to recognize that there are answers to every
question, even if the answer is "I don't know." Now that we
have considered some principles that should underlie our interactions with individuals of other faiths, let us turn to ways we
might respond to specific questions or objections.

1. How can the Latter-day Saints justify having additional books
of scripture?

In a seminar on biblical studies I attended at an eastern university years ago, the instructor emphasized for at least two hours
that the word *canon*—referring, of course, to the biblical books
that are generally included in the Judaeo-Christian collection—
was the "rule of faith," the standard against which we measure
what is acceptable in belief and practice. He also stated that the
canon, if the word meant anything at all, was "closed, fixed, set,
and established." He must have stressed those words at least ten
times as he wrote them on the blackboard again and again. At

the next session on this topic the instructor seemed a bit uneasy. I remember thinking that something must be wrong. Without warning, he stopped what he was doing, banged his fist on the table, turned to me, and said, "Mr. Millet, will you please explain to this group the Latter-day Saint concept of canon, given your people's acceptance of the Book of Mormon and other books of scripture beyond the Bible?"

Startled, I paused for several seconds, looked up at the blackboard, saw the now very familiar words under *canon*, and finally answered, "Well, I suppose you could say that the Latter-day Saints believe the canon of scripture is *open, flexible,* and *expanding.*" The class then had a really fascinating discussion!

Joseph Smith loved the Bible. Through pondering upon certain verses in the epistle of James, he felt directed to call upon God in prayer. Most of his sermons, writings, and letters are laced with quotations or paraphrasing summaries of biblical passages and precepts from both the Old and New Testaments. The Prophet once remarked that we can "see God's own handwriting in the sacred volume: and he who reads it oftenest will like it best."[1] From his earliest days, however, he did not believe the Bible was complete or that religious difficulties could necessarily be resolved by turning to the Old or the New Testament (Joseph Smith–History 1:12).

"From what we can draw from the Scriptures relative to the teaching of heaven," the Prophet stated, "we are induced to think that much instruction has been given to man since the beginning which we do not possess now. . . . We have what we have, and the Bible contains what it does contain: but to say that God never said anything more to man than is there recorded, would be saying at once that we have at last received a revelation: for it must require one to advance thus far."[2]

In a letter to his uncle, Silas Smith, Joseph wrote in 1833 of the need for continual direction through prophets: "Seeing that the Lord has never given the world to understand by anything heretofore revealed that he had ceased forever to speak to his creatures when sought unto in a proper manner, why should it be thought a thing incredible that he should be pleased to speak again in these last days for their salvation? Perhaps you may be surprised at this assertion that I should say for the salvation of his creatures in these last days, since we have already in our possession a vast volume of his word [the Bible] which he has previously given. But you will admit that the word spoken to Noah was not sufficient for Abraham. . . . Isaac, the promised seed, was not required to rest his hope upon the promises made to his father Abraham but was privileged with the assurance of his approbation in the sight of Heaven by the direct voice of the Lord to him. . . .

"I have no doubt but that the holy prophets and apostles and saints in ancient days were saved in the Kingdom of God. . . . I may believe that Enoch walked with God. I may believe that Abraham communed with God and conversed with angels. . . . I may believe that Elijah was taken to Heaven in a chariot of fire with fiery horses. I may believe that the saints saw the Lord and conversed with him face to face after his resurrection. I may believe that the Hebrew Church came to Mount Zion and unto the city of the living God, the Heavenly Jerusalem, and to an innumerable company of angels. I may believe that they looked into Eternity and saw the Judge of all, and Jesus the Mediator of the new covenant; but will all this purchase an assurance for me, or waft me to the regions of Eternal day with my garments spotless, pure, and white? Or, must I not rather obtain for myself, by my own faith and diligence, in keeping the commandments of the Lord, an assurance of salvation for myself? And have I not an equal privilege with the ancient saints? And will not the Lord hear my prayers, and listen to my cries, as soon [as] he ever did to theirs, if I come to him in the manner they did? Or is he a respecter of persons?"[3]

Occasionally we hear certain Latter-day Saint teachings described as *unbiblical* or a particular doctrine as being *contradictory* to the Bible. Let's be clear on this matter. The Bible is one of the books within our standard works, and thus our doctrines and practices are in harmony with the Bible. There are times, of course, when latter-day revelation provides clarification or enhancement of the intended meaning in the Bible. Addition to the canon is not, however, the same as rejection of the canon. Supplementation is not the same as contradiction. All of the prophets and the Savior himself were sent to bring new light and knowledge to the world; in many cases, new scripture came as a result of their ministry. That new scripture did not invalidate what went before, nor did it close the door to subsequent revelation. We feel deep gratitude for the holy scriptures, but we do not worship scripture. Nor do we feel it appropriate to set bounds to the works and ways of the Almighty, to tell God, essentially, "Thus far and no more." As the Lord declared through Nephi, "Wherefore, because that ye have a Bible ye need not suppose that it contains all my words; neither need ye suppose that I have not caused more to be written" (2 Nephi 29:10). In short, we believe God has spoken through modern prophets, restored his everlasting gospel, delivered new truths, and commissioned us to make them known to the world. We feel it would be unchristian *not* to share what has been communicated to us.

Persons of other faiths sometimes cite scriptural warnings against adding to or taking away from the Bible. The passages in the Old Testament that warn against such things (Deuteronomy 4:2; 12:32) are warnings against adding to the books of Moses, the Pentateuch. They certainly could not refer to adding to the Old Testament in general, or else we could not in good conscience accept the thirty-four books that follow the Pentateuch. Furthermore, the warning attached to the end of the Revelation of John is a warning against adding to or taking away from "the words of the prophecy of this book" (Revelation 22:18), namely, the Apocalypse. Most important, Latter-day Saints believe that these warnings have to do with the condemnation associated with a man—an uninspired man, a man not called of God—taking upon himself the responsibility to add to or take from the canon of scripture. It is God's right to speak beyond what he has spoken already (as he certainly did in the person and messages and works of Jesus himself), and Latter-day Saints feel that God directs and empowers his children as need arises. Nowhere does the Bible itself declare that God will no longer speak directly to his children or add to past scripture.

2. Do the Latter-day Saints mistrust the Bible?

One of our Articles of Faith does indeed place a bit of a qualifier upon our feelings toward the Bible, because we believe the Bible to be the word of God "as far as it is translated correctly" (Article of Faith 8). We believe that errors in the Bible have occurred through the centuries (1 Nephi 13:20–29),[4] but we also believe that the essential message of the Bible is intact and that the lessons and precepts taught therein are both timely and timeless. As Latter-day Saints we do not feel it necessary to believe that every word from Genesis to Revelation represents a direct dictation from God or that the Bible now reads as it has always read in order to have sufficient confidence in the message of that sacred volume.

Errors in the Bible should not tarnish its image, for there is still much within its covers that is beautiful and wholesome and ennobling. Our duty, President George Q. Cannon reminded us, is to engender faith in the Bible: "As our duty is to create faith in the word of God in the mind of the young student, we scarcely think that object is best attained by making the mistakes of translators the more prominent part of our teachings. Even children have their doubts, but it is not our business to encourage those doubts. Doubts never convert; negations seldom convince. . . .

"The clause in the Articles of Faith regarding mistakes in the translation of the Bible was never inserted to encourage us to spend our time in searching out and studying those errors, but to emphasize the idea that it is the truth and the truth only that the Church of Jesus Christ of Latter-day Saints accepts, no matter where it is found."[5]

3. Why do the Latter-day Saints deny that the Bible has come to us without flaw or error?

There is misunderstanding in the minds of both Latter-day Saints and more traditional Christians in regard to scriptural inerrancy, the idea that the scriptures are flawless, without error. My own reading and long conversations with other Christian friends have shown me that the notion of scriptural inerrancy is not especially helpful in evaluating the truthfulness of *today's* Bible. Rather, it means that the original autographs—the scriptural records as written by the apostles and prophets of old— were without error. Perhaps scriptural inerrancy could be established if we had the original documents in our possession, but we do not. What we have are copies of copies of copies of copies of copies. We love the Bible, we treasure its truths, and we seek to emulate the lives of those who were true and faithful in their own day and time, particularly the Lord Jesus Christ himself. But for us it is not so much the written word as it is the living Word, who quickened the minds and souls of those who have recorded holy writ.

4. *What are examples of truths that you feel have been lost from scripture?*

Some examples of plain and precious truths lost wholly or in part from scripture might include the following:

- The nature of God the Father—that he is an exalted Man of Holiness, a corporeal being;
- God the Father, Jesus Christ, and the Holy Ghost are separate and distinct beings and three Gods;
- Christ's eternal gospel—the knowledge that Christian prophets have declared Christian doctrines and administered Christian ordinances since the days of Adam and that the ancient prophets in the Old Testament were acquainted with the plan of salvation and of the redemptive role of Jesus Christ;
- The infinite and eternal nature of Christ's atonement;
- The premortal existence of human beings;
- All persons are literally the children of God, spirit sons and daughters of the same Eternal Father;
- All individuals have within them the capacity, through the transforming powers of Jesus Christ and by the proper exercise of their moral agency, to acquire divine attributes;
- God has a plan, a great plan of happiness, a system of salvation whereby his children may progress in light and truth;
- Life and work within the postmortal spirit world;
- The kingdoms of glory hereafter; and
- The necessity of priesthood authority and saving ordinances (sacraments).

Some of these verities can be found in the Bible, but because they are not amplified or explained there, some of their meanings and doctrinal implications remain unclear, especially without the aid of the restored gospel.

5. Is it true that the Latter-day Saints tend to read the Bible through the lens of their other scriptures?

Just as the Former-day Saints in New Testament times read the Old Testament with their eyes wide open to the person, powers, passion, death, and resurrection of Jesus Christ, so do we as Latter-day Saints read the Bible through the lens of Restoration scriptures. Just as we recognize the fulfillment of messianic prophecies in Zechariah or Micah or Isaiah in the teachings and life of Jesus, so we appreciate more fully the marvelous doctrine of salvation by grace through the clarifying teachings of Nephi and Jacob and Moroni; to make sense of the rather cryptic verses in Romans 11 regarding the grafting of the branches of the wild olive tree through studying carefully the more complete allegory of Zenos in Jacob 5; to have our minds expanded upon the Savior's words concerning "many mansions" hereafter through reading the vision of the glories (D&C 76); to learn the import of Peter's words concerning Christ preaching to the "spirits in prison" through pondering President Joseph F. Smith's vision of the redemption of the dead (D&C 138); to know just what Adam and Eve and Enoch understood about God, Christ, and the plan of salvation through reading Joseph Smith's translation of the early chapters of Genesis (Moses 4–7); to gain even deeper insight to the Abrahamic covenant (described in Genesis 13, 15, 17) through reading the Prophet Joseph's translation of the Egyptian papyri (Abraham 2:8–11); and so on. The greatest commentary on scripture is scripture, and it is our duty to follow the example of the Master Teacher, who "expounded all the scriptures in one" (3 Nephi 23:14; compare Luke 24:27).

6. *Why do the Latter-day Saints continue to use the King James Version of the Bible when there are so many useful, easy-to-read, updated translations?*

As the years have gone by, I have come to treasure the King James Bible more and more. Its translators sought to produce a version of the Bible that was both accurate and spiritually satisfying. Although I occasionally do find it useful to turn to another translation for a plainer rendering of certain passages, I personally do not feel the same sense of reverence and awe for the holy word when I read other versions. Christian scholar Alister McGrath has written that "in popular Christian culture, the King James translation is seen to possess a dignity and authority that modern translations somehow fail to convey." Further, "the glory of the King James Bible was that the English language was raised to new heights by being put to the service of this supreme goal—the rendering in English of the words and deeds of God."[6]

"Many versions of the Bible are available today," stated the First Presidency in 1992. "Unfortunately, no original manuscripts of any portion of the Bible are available for comparison to determine the most accurate version. However, the Lord has revealed clearly the doctrines of the gospel in these latter days. The most reliable way to measure the accuracy of any biblical passage is not by comparing different texts, but by comparison with the Book of Mormon and modern-day revelations.

"While other Bible versions may be easier to read than the King James Version, in doctrinal matters latter-day revelation supports the King James Version in preference to other English translations. All of the Presidents of the Church, beginning with the Prophet Joseph Smith, have supported the King James

Version by encouraging its continued use in the Church. In light of all the above, it is the English language Bible used by The Church of Jesus Christ of Latter-day Saints.

"The LDS edition of the Bible (1979) contains the King James Version supplemented and clarified by footnotes, study aids, and cross-references to the Book of Mormon, the Doctrine and Covenants, and the Pearl of Great Price. These four books are the standard works of the Church. We encourage all members to have their own copies of the complete standard works and to use them prayerfully in regular personal and family study, and in Church meetings and assignments."[7]

7. *Because the Latter-day Saints have other books of scripture, do they often pay less attention to the Bible and thus are less acquainted with the Bible than they should be?*

The Bible is one of the books in our scriptural canon, and it is thus one of the books we are encouraged to study, ponder, pray over, and even memorize portions of. As a result of the correlated, four-year cycle of scripture study in the Church, combined with the excellent work of the Church Educational System, the Latter-day Saints as a people have become more scripturally literate than ever before—and that includes knowledge of the Old and the New Testament. I see it in Gospel Doctrine classes as well as in my work as a professor of religion at BYU. Students today are many times better prepared to know their Lord and defend his gospel than any generation heretofore.

This change is in large measure a fulfillment of a prophecy uttered by Elder Boyd K. Packer in 1982: "With the passing of years, these scriptures [the 1979 LDS edition of the King James Bible and the 1981 edition of the Book of Mormon, Doctrine and Covenants, and Pearl of Great Price] will produce successive generations of faithful Christians who know the Lord Jesus Christ and are disposed to obey His will.

"The older generation has been raised without them, but there is another generation growing up. The revelations will be opened to them as to no other in the history of the world. Into their hands now are placed the sticks of Joseph [Book of Mormon] and of Judah [Bible]. They will develop a gospel scholarship beyond that which their forebears could achieve. They will have the testimony that Jesus is the Christ and be competent to proclaim Him and to defend Him."[8]

8. *Doesn't the Book of Mormon's seeming to address itself to so many religious questions of Joseph Smith's day suggest that it is a product of the nineteenth century and not an ancient text?*

We are given little indication in the biblical record that the prophet-writers delivered and preserved their messages for any day other than their own. Yet there is no doubt that Isaiah, Jeremiah, Ezekiel, Daniel, Malachi, Peter, Paul, John, and others spoke of the distant future and that by the power of the Spirit they saw and described the doings of peoples of another time and place. Their words were given to the people of their own time, although their words will find application and fulfillment in a future day. Never do we see a particular prophet from the stick of Judah addressing himself directly to those who will one day read his pronouncements.

How very different is the Book of Mormon. It was prepared and preserved by men with seeric vision who wrote and spoke to us; they saw and knew our day and addressed themselves to specific issues that people in the last days would confront. The poignant words of Moroni alert us to the contemporary relevance of the Book of Mormon: "Behold, I speak unto you as if ye were present, and yet ye are not. But behold, Jesus Christ hath shown you unto me, and I know your doing" (Mormon 8:35). Later Moroni said: "Behold, I speak unto you as though I spake from the dead; for I know that ye shall have my words" (Mormon 9:30). In the words of President Ezra Taft Benson, the Book of Mormon "was written for our day. The Nephites never had the book; neither did the Lamanites of ancient times. It was meant for us. Mormon wrote near the end of the Nephite civilization. Under the inspiration of God, who sees all things from the beginning, he abridged centuries of records, choosing the stories, speeches, and events that would be most helpful to us. . . .

"If they saw our day, and chose those things which would be of greatest worth to us, is not that how we should study the Book of Mormon? We should constantly ask ourselves, 'Why did the Lord inspire Mormon (or Moroni or Alma) to include that in his record? What lesson can I learn from that to help me live in this day and age?'"[9]

Do I desire to know how to handle wayward children, how to deal justly yet mercifully with transgressors, how to bear pure testimony, how to teach and preach in such a manner that people cannot go away unaffected, how to detect the enemies of Christ and how to withstand those who seek to destroy my faith, how to discern and expose secret combinations that seek to impede the work of the Lamb of God, how to deal properly with persecution and anti-Mormonism, and how to establish Zion? Then I must search and study the Book of Mormon.

Do I desire to know more about how to avoid pride and the perils of the prosperity cycle; how to avoid priestcraft and acquire and embody charity, the pure love of Christ; how my sins may be remitted and how I can know when they have been forgiven; how to retain a remission of sins from day to day; how to come unto Christ, receive his holy name, partake of his goodness and love, be sanctified by his Spirit, and eventually be sealed to him? Do I desire to know how to prepare for the Second Coming of the Son of Man? Then I must search and study the Book of Mormon. This volume of holy writ is without peer. It is the most relevant and pertinent book available to humankind today.

9. Why does the Book of Mormon contain so many direct quotations from the King James Version of the Bible?

The Book of Mormon is translation literature. That is, while the Prophet Joseph Smith enjoyed the divine assistance of the Urim and Thummim as well as the direction of the Holy Spirit, he was still required to use the language with which he was most familiar, namely, English. The instructions to Joseph Smith and Oliver Cowdery in Doctrine and Covenants 9:7–9 suggest that more was involved in the process of translation and transcription than simply reading the translation and dictating it to the scribe. Rather, a strenuous mental process was involved. Many have asked, for example, why the book of Jacob would end with the words, "Brethren, adieu." The word *adieu* is a French word that means "good-bye" or "until tomorrow." Did Jacob speak French? Of course not. Joseph the translator clearly drew upon a word with which he was familiar, a word that conveyed well the concept he perceived on the golden plates.

King James English was the scriptural language most familiar to Joseph Smith and the people of his day. Thus, it is the language in which both the Book of Mormon and the Doctrine and Covenants are written. It may be, although it is not known for certain, that Joseph and his scribe had access to a King James Bible during the translation of the Book of Mormon. Whenever the Prophet sensed that the language on the golden plates (both in the Isaiah chapters and the sermon in 3 Nephi 12–14) was close to the wording of the King James Translation, he chose to

GETTING AT THE TRUTH

use the words of the Bible. Joseph was not simply copying every-thing word for word; scores of words are different.

10. Does DNA research prove that the Book of Mormon could not be an actual history of an ancient Hebrew people?

Recent DNA research has seemed to point toward Native Americans being of Asiatic ancestry, whereas the Book of Mormon claims its peoples came from the Middle East in 600 B.C. and would thus have a different genetic signature. Brigham Young University biology professor Michael F. Whiting, a specialist in molecular systematics who frequently evaluates proposals involving DNA research for the National Science Foundation, has offered the following ideas for consideration:

- DNA analysis has proven a remarkable tool in recent years, but it cannot properly address itself to a faith claim, which the Book of Mormon certainly is. The truthfulness of the message of the Book of Mormon, or even its origins, cannot really be fully explained, explained away, supported, or dismissed by scientific proofs, any more than we could prove scientifically many of the faith claims (miraculous events) in the New Testament: that Jesus healed the sick, raised the dead, multiplied fish and loaves, or was resurrected himself.
- The DNA "evidence" put forward is not based upon a particular study; there is no study, only interpolations of and extrapolations from others' work that had nothing to do with testing Book of Mormon truth claims.
- This critique of the Book of Mormon presupposes a kind of "global colonization" of the Book of Mormon peoples—that they remained a separate and distinct people for more than a thousand years and thus no "genetic drift" occurred during that millennium. In contrast, many, if not

— 100 —

most, Book of Mormon scholars believe in a "local colonization" process, that is, when the colony of Lehi came to America, there were already indigenous peoples in the land (of unknown genetic origin), peoples the Nephites identified as the "other guys," or Lamanites, with whom they intermarried over time, thus precluding a single Lehite DNA strain to be identified, isolated, followed, and studied.

Professor Whiting declared that he "would be just as critical of someone who rose up and said, 'I now have DNA evidence proving the Book of Mormon is true.' The science is tough, and the answers do not come unambiguously."[10]

11. Don't recent translations of the so-called "Joseph Smith papyri" by experts demonstrate that the book of Abraham is a hoax?

In the summer of 1835 members of the Church purchased from Michael Chandler four mummies and two or more papyrus scrolls that had been discovered in Egypt by a man named Antonio Lebolo. The Prophet Joseph Smith showed little interest in the mummies but was fascinated by the papyri. Through the use of the Urim and Thummim and with W. W. Phelps and Oliver Cowdery as scribes, Brother Joseph began to translate "some of the characters or hieroglyphics, and much to our joy found that one of the rolls contained the writings of Abraham, another the writings of Joseph of Egypt, etc.,—a more full account of which will appear in its place, as I proceed to examine or unfold them. Truly we can say, the Lord is beginning to reveal the abundance of peace and truth."[11]

In his journal entry of 1 October 1835, the Prophet recorded that "during the research, the principles of astronomy as understood by Father Abraham and the ancients unfolded to our understanding."[12] Oliver Cowdery reported that "when the translation of these valuable documents will be completed, I am unable to say; neither can I give you a probable idea how large volumes they will make; but judging from their size, and the comprehensiveness of the language, one might reasonably expect to see sufficient to develop much upon the mighty acts of the ancient men of God, and of his dealing with the children of men when they saw him face to face."[13] In 1838 Anson Call visited the Prophet in Far West, Missouri. Joseph invited him in and said, " 'Sit down and we will read to you from the translations of the Book of Abraham.' Oliver Cowdery then read until he was tired when Thomas Marsh read, *making altogether about two hours*. I was much interested in the work."[14] The book of Abraham and the three facsimiles, as we now have them in our Pearl of Great Price, were published in the *Times and Seasons* in March 1842. Nearly a year later, in the 1 February 1843 issue, *Times and Seasons* editor John Taylor encouraged the Saints to renew their subscriptions to the paper, adding: "We would further state that *we had the promise of Br. Joseph, to furnish us with further extracts from the Book of Abraham*."[15]

The history of the papyri after the death of the Prophet is sketchy. The Egyptian relics were kept by Lucy Mack Smith until her death and were then sold by Emma Smith Bidamon to a Mr. A. Combs. Combs sold two of the mummies with some papyri to the St. Louis Museum in 1856, and in 1863 they were sold to the Chicago Museum (later renamed the Woods Museum). It has generally been assumed that all of the papyri were destroyed in the great Chicago fire in 1871. In 1967, however, it was announced that Dr. Aziz Atiya, a professor of Middle Eastern Studies at the University of Utah, had found eleven papyrus fragments, including Facsimile 1, in the New York Metropolitan Museum of Art. Not being a Latter-day Saint himself (he was a Coptic Christian) but being somewhat familiar with

Latter-day Saint culture and the Pearl of Great Price, Dr. Atiya recognized Facsimile 1 and made contact with Church leaders, who eventually acquired the papyrus fragments.

Committed Latter-day Saints and critics of the faith alike were intrigued with what would come of the find. The latter group exulted that once and for all the book of Abraham could be exposed as a figment of Joseph Smith's fertile imagination. The translation of the eleven fragments and the facsimile by trained Egyptologists revealed parts of the ancient Egyptian Book of Breathings, an excerpt of the larger Book of the Dead, which are actually funerary texts, material associated with the burial and future state of the dead. In other words, the fragments presumably had nothing to do with the person and work of Abraham. The late H. Donl Peterson, professor of ancient scripture at Brigham Young University and dedicated student of the book of Abraham, replied: "The Book of Abraham and Joseph papyri were described as 'Beautifully written on papyrus, with black, and a small part red, ink or paint, in perfect preservation.' The eleven fragments recovered from the Metropolitan Musuem of Art in New York City do not fit that description at all. What was discovered was Facsimile One and some other fragments unrelated to the published account of the present Book of Abraham. They were part of the original scrolls once owned by Joseph Smith but not directly related to the Abrahamic text. The partial text of the Book of Breathings returned to the Church in 1967 was not the text for the Book of Abraham."

Professor Peterson said that the book of Abraham "was not finished. In fact, it was hardly begun. The Book of Abraham was a lengthy record. . . . Oliver Cowdery spoke of volumes necessary to contain it. Only two short installments were published during Joseph Smith's lifetime, although more was promised. Had not Joseph Smith's last 16 months been so turbulent, no doubt more

of the translation would have been forthcoming, as he had promised. We have but a small fraction of a rather lengthy record."[16]

"Is the Book of Abraham true?" Elder Bruce R. McConkie
asked. "Yes, but it is not complete; it stops almost in midair.
Would that the Prophet had gone on in his translation or revelation, as the case may be."[17]

12. Which is more important to the Latter-day Saints—scripture or prophets?

It is important for us as Latter-day Saints to ask why so many
in the Christian world argue for scriptural inerrancy and for the
sufficiency of the Bible. The answer is that the Bible is all they
have. They have a closed canon, no living prophets, no institutional revelation beyond the Bible. Because the Bible is all they
have, it becomes the source of their authority, their doctrine, and
their commission to teach and preach. Without it they have
nothing. It is a bit like Samson fighting the Philistines with the
jawbone of an ass. If it is all you have, you use it, but it is certainly not the ultimate weapon. The ultimate weapon is the
power of God that enabled Samson to wield his weapon so effectively. It is that power we seek.

Stone, leaves, bark, skins, wood, metals, baked clay, pot-
sherds, and papyrus were all used anciently to record inspired
messages. Our concern with the ancients is not the perfection
with which such messages were recorded but with the inspiration of the message. More important, we are interested that the
heavens were open to them and that they had such messages
to record. Knowing as we do that God is the same yesterday,
today, and forever, that he spoke to them, however poorly they
preserved it, witnesses that he can speak to us. After all, the Bible
is only ink on paper until the Spirit of God manifests its true
meaning to us; if we have obtained that, what need do we have

to quibble, for example, over the Bible's suitability as a history or science text? The Bible does not pretend to have the answers to all questions. Those who claim it does make a claim for the Bible that it does not make for itself. In fact, the Bible continuously directs its readers to implore the heavens for knowledge and understanding beyond what it contains. Elder Dallin H. Oaks has taught: "What makes us different from most other Christians in the way we read and use the Bible and other scriptures is our belief in continuing revelation. For us, the scriptures are not the ultimate source of knowledge, but what precedes the ultimate source. The ultimate knowledge comes by revelation."[18]

We love the scriptures, but ours is a living Church; not all of the mind and will of the Almighty can or should be written down. Truly, "notwithstanding those things which are written, it always has been given to the elders of my church from the beginning, and ever shall be, to conduct all meetings as they are directed and guided by the Holy Spirit" (D&C 46:2). If God is going to make anything known to his covenant people or to the world, he will do so through his living prophets (Amos 3:7). The scriptures guide our conduct and our beliefs, and the teachings of prophets will be consistent with the eternal principles contained in scripture. As President Spencer W. Kimball observed, however, "There are those who would assume that with the printing and binding of these sacred records [the standard works], that would be the 'end of the prophets.' But again we testify to the world that revelation continues and that the vaults and files of the Church contain these revelations which come month to month and day to day."[19] Indeed, "the last word has not been spoken on any subject. Streams of living water shall yet flow from the Eternal Spring who is the source of all truth."[20]

CHAPTER 6

GOD AND MAN

The first vision of Joseph Smith represents to Latter-day Saints the beginning of the revelation of God to man in this final dispensation. Knowledge pertaining to the nature of God—his character, personality, divine attributes, powers, and purposes—has been made known through latter-day prophets, and some of this knowledge obviously stands in contrast to what many in the Christian world believe about God and about man's relationship to Deity. The following are a few questions that are often asked about the Latter-day Saint doctrine of God, the Godhead, and man's relationship to that divine presidency.

1. Do the Latter-day Saints really believe in the Fall? Why do they not believe in human depravity, as most other Christians do?

On the whole, the Latter-day Saint perspective on the Fall of Adam and Eve is optimistic when compared with views held by traditional Christians, who generally believe in the depravity of humankind. As Latter-day Saints, we believe that Adam and Eve went into the Garden to fall and that their fall was as much a part of the foreordained plan of the Father as was the Atonement. Modern scripture repeatedly speaks of the actions of Adam and Eve in Eden as a transgression, not a sin (2 Nephi 2:22; 9:6; Article of Faith 2). We echo Lehi's words: "Adam fell that men might be; and men are, that they might have joy" (2 Nephi

2:25). Elder Orson F. Whitney taught that "the fall had a two-fold direction—downward, yet forward. It brought man into the world and set his feet upon progression's highway."[1]

On the other hand, we believe that the Fall does take a toll on all of humankind, both temporal and spiritual. We as Latter-day Saints do not believe in the traditional Christian view of human depravity, but we do believe that "since man had fallen he could not merit anything of himself" (Alma 22:14). The Fall created a separation between man and God, a chasm that could be bridged only by and through the infinite and eternal atoning sacrifice of Jesus Christ. It is clear from the scriptures, ancient and modern, that we cannot forgive our own sins, change our own nature, raise ourselves from the dead, or glorify ourselves hereafter. Such is the work of a God, even the work of the Son of God.

2. If God has a physical body, as the Latter-day Saints claim, is he not limited?

We believe that all humankind are created in the image of God. We believe that God is more than a force, more than a divine influence, more than a great unmoved mover. We believe, further, that he possesses all the attributes of godliness in perfection. That God has a physical body (D&C 130:22) is one of the most important of all truths restored in this dispensation: it is inextricably linked to such doctrines as the immortality of the soul, the literal resurrection, eternal marriage, and the continuation of the family unit into eternity. In his corporeal, or physical, nature, God can be in only one place at a time. His divine nature is such, however, that through his Holy Spirit, his glory, his power, and his influence fill the immensity of space. His Holy Spirit is the means by which God is omnipresent and through which law and light and life are extended to us (D&C 88:6–13).

The Father's physical body does not limit his capacity or detract one whit from his infinite holiness, any more than Christ's resurrected body did (Luke 24; John 20–21). The risen Lord said of himself: "All power is given unto me in heaven and in earth" (Matthew 28:18).

Interestingly, according to research by David Paulsen of the Brigham Young University philosophy department, the idea of God's corporeality was taught in the early Christian church into the fourth and fifth centuries, before being lost to the knowledge of the people.[2]

Scholars of other faiths have commented on the possibility of God's corporeality. James L. Kugel, professor of Hebrew literature at Harvard, wrote that it is not necessarily the case that "what our religions say nowadays about God is what people have always believed." Indeed, some of scholars' "most basic assumptions about God," including the idea that "He has no body but exists everywhere simultaneously," are "not articulated in the most ancient parts of the Bible." Kugel observed that "biblical narratives did not like to speak of God actually appearing to human beings directly and conversing with them face-to-face. The reason was not that God in those days was thought to be invisible, and certainly not that He was (as later philosophers and theologians were to claim) altogether spiritual and therefore had no body to be seen. Rather, God in the Bible is not usually seen by human beings for an entirely different reason, especially in the earliest parts: catching sight of Him was believed to be extremely dangerous." Further, "the same God who buttonholes the patriarchs and speaks to Moses face-to-face is perceived in later times as a huge, cosmic deity—not necessarily invisible or lacking a body, but so huge as to surpass our own capacities of apprehension, almost our imagination." In time the God who spoke to Moses directly "became an embarrassment to later theologians.

It is, they said, really the great, universal God" who is "omniscient and omnipresent and utterly unphysical." Kugel asked,
"Indeed, does not the eventual emergence of Christianity—in
particular Nicene Christianity, with its doctrine of the Trinity—
likewise represent in its own way an attempt to fill the gap left
by the God of Old," the God known to the ancient prophets?[3]

Evangelical scholar Clark Pinnock has written that if we "are
to take biblical metaphors seriously, is God in some way embodied? Critics will be quick to say that, although there are expressions of this idea in the Bible, they are not to be taken literally.
But I do not believe that the idea is as foreign to the Bible's view
of God as we have assumed. In tradition, God is thought to
function primarily as a disembodied spirit but this is scarcely a
biblical idea. For example, Israel is called to hear God's word and
gaze on his glory and beauty. Human beings are said to be
embodied creatures created in the image of God. Is there perhaps something in God that corresponds with embodiment?
Having a body is certainly not a negative thing because it makes
it possible for us to be agents. Perhaps God's agency would be
easier to envisage if he were in some way corporeal. Add to that
the fact that in the theophanies of the Old Testament God
encounters humans in the form of a man. . . . Add to that the
fact that God took on a body in the incarnation and Christ has
taken that body with him into glory. It seems to me that the
Bible does not think of God as formless."[4]

3. *How can Latter-day Saints believe in a God with a physical
   body of flesh and bones when the scriptures clearly teach that
   "God is a spirit" (John 4:24)?*

We as Latter-day Saints believe what we believe about the
corporeal nature of God as a result of modern revelation. As early
as 1830 Joseph Smith recorded the following, which is now in

the Pearl of Great Price: "In the day that God created man, in the likeness of God made he him; in the image of his own body, male and female, created he them, and blessed them" (Moses 6:8–9; emphasis added). In 1841 the Prophet declared: "That which is without body, parts and passions is nothing. There is no other God in heaven but that God who has flesh and bones."[5] In April 1843 Joseph taught that "the Father has a body of flesh and bones as tangible as man's; the Son also; but the Holy Ghost has not a body of flesh and bones, but is a personage of Spirit" (D&C 130:22). Two months later he explained: "As the Father hath power in Himself, so hath the Son power in Himself . . . so He has a body of His own. . . . Each one [God and Christ] will be in His own body; and yet the sectarian world believe the body of the Son is identical with the Father's."[6]

Elder Bruce R. McConkie wrote that the statement "God is a spirit" (John 4:24) has been "interpreted by the Christian world to mean that God is a spirit essence that fills all space, has no form or substance, and dwells in human hearts. It might properly be said that 'God is a Spirit' if by that is meant that he has a spiritual or resurrected body in harmony with Paul's statement relative to the resurrection that the body 'is sown a natural body; it is raised a spiritual body.'"[7] The word *spiritual,* as used in the New Testament and in Latter-day Saint scripture, means immortal, not subject to death. Thus, the mortal body is temporal and corrupt, whereas the resurrected, immortal body is incorruptible and spiritual, meaning that it is no longer subject to the pulls and passions of life and the ever-present reality of physical death (1 Corinthians 15:44). One Book of Mormon prophet affirmed that "this mortal body is raised to an immortal body, that is from death, even from the first death unto life, that they can die no more; their spirits uniting with their bodies, never to be divided; thus the whole becoming spiritual and immortal, that they can no more see corruption" (Alma 11:45). Likewise modern revelation, in speaking of the resurrection of individuals, points out that "notwithstanding they die, they also shall rise again, a spiritual body" (D&C 88:27).

Finally, the correct translation of John 4:24 is not "God is a spirit," but rather "God is spirit" (NKJV, NIV, NRSV, NEB). That is to say, God is approached and known in spiritual ways, or he is known not at all; indeed, God stands revealed, or he remains forever unknown. Because we are made up of both body and spirit, and because our spirit is the real, inner, eternal part of ourselves, modern revelation teaches that "man is spirit" as well (D&C 93:33). "For what man knoweth the things of a man, save the spirit of man which is in him? even so the things of God knoweth no man, but the Spirit of God" (1 Corinthians 2:11).

4. *What do Latter-day Saints really mean when they state that God is a man? How can he then be, as the scriptures declare, "from everlasting to everlasting"?*

A careful search of the scriptures, ancient and modern, shows that such phrases as "from everlasting to everlasting" or "the same yesterday, today, and forever" (e.g., Psalm 102:27; Hebrews 1:12; 13:8; 1 Nephi 10:18–19; 2 Nephi 27:23; Alma 7:20; Mormon 9:8–11, 19; Moroni 8:18; 10:7; D&C 3:2; 20:12, 17; 35:1) clearly refer to God's divine attributes—his love, justice, constancy, and willingness to bless his children. As Latter-day Saints, we believe that God is a Man, a Man of Holiness (Moses 6:57), an exalted and immortal being who has a body of flesh and bones. President Joseph Fielding Smith explained that "from eternity to eternity means from the spirit existence through the probation which we are in, and then back again to the eternal existence which will follow. Surely this is everlasting, for when we receive the resurrection, we will never die. We all existed in the first eternity. I think I can say of myself and others, we are from eternity; and we will be to eternity everlasting, if we receive the exaltation."[8]

My colleague Stephen Robinson has pointed out further that "in both Hebrew and Greek the words for 'eternity' (*'olam* and *aion,* respectively) denote neither an endless linear time nor a state outside of time, but rather 'an age,' an 'epoch,' 'a long time,' 'world,' or some other such term—even 'a lifetime,' or 'a generation'—always a measurable *period* of time rather than *endless* time or timelessness. . . .

"It was only in post-biblical times and mainly under the influence of Greek philosophy that the concept of eternity (or forever) as endless time, or timelessness, or as a state outside of time replaced the original meaning of a period, or of an age."[9]

5. Do the Latter-day Saints believe that man may become as God? Isn't this idea blasphemous?

Jesus Christ is an unselfish Being. He is a glorified, exalted, perfected personage who also yearns to forgive our sins and purify our hearts, who delights to honor those who serve him in righteousness and in truth (D&C 76:5). That is, he is not possessive of his powers, nor does he hesitate to dispense spiritual gifts or share divine attributes.

Joseph Smith taught that all who keep God's commandments "shall grow up from grace to grace, and become heirs of the heavenly kingdom, and joint heirs with Jesus Christ; possessing the same mind, being transformed into the same image or likeness." Truly, "as the Son partakes of the fullness of the Father through the Spirit, so the saints are, by the same Spirit, to be partakers of the same fullness, to enjoy the same glory; for as the Father and Son are one, so, in like manner, the saints are to be one in them. Through the love of the Father, the mediation of

Jesus Christ, and the gift of the Holy Spirit, they are to be heirs of God, and joint heirs with Jesus Christ."[10]

God is the Father of the spirits of all humankind (Numbers 16:22; 27:16), the source of light and truth, the embodiment of all godly attributes and gifts, and the supreme power and intelligence over all things. On the one hand, we worship a divine Being with whom we can identify. That is to say, his infinity does not preclude his immediacy or his intimacy. "In the day that God created man," our Latter-day Saint scripture attests, "in the likeness of God made he him; in the image of his own body, male and female, created he them" (Moses 6:8–9). We believe that God is not simply a spirit influence, a force in the universe, or the Great First Cause; when we pray, "Our Father which art in heaven" (Matthew 6:9), we mean what we say. We believe God is comprehendible, knowable, approachable, and, like his Beloved Son, "touched with the feeling of our infirmities" (Hebrews 4:15). On the other hand, our God is God. There is no knowledge of which the Father is ignorant and no power he does not possess (1 Nephi 7:12; 2 Nephi 9:20; Mosiah 4:9; Alma 26:35; Helaman 9:41; Ether 3:4).

We come to the earth to take a physical body, to be schooled and gain experiences here that we could not have in the premortal life, our "first estate" (Jude 1:6; Abraham 3:26). We strive to keep the commandments and grow in faith and spiritual graces until we are prepared to go where God and Christ are. The Doctrine and Covenants teaches: "That which is of God is light; and he that receiveth light, and continueth in God, receiveth more light; and that light groweth brighter and brighter until the perfect day" (D&C 50:24). That "perfect day" is the resurrection, the day when spirit and body are inseparably united in immortal glory. That is, those "who are quickened by a portion of the celestial glory [in this life] shall then [in the resurrection] receive of the same, even a fulness" (D&C 88:29). Another place in the Doctrine and Covenants instructs us that those who come unto Christ, follow his path to the Father, and thus realize the fruits of true worship are empowered to "come unto the Father in my name, and in due time receive of his fulness" (D&C 93:19). That is what Latter-day Saints call gaining eternal life, which consists in being *with* God; in addition, it entails being *like* God. A study of Christian history reveals that the doctrine of the deification of man was taught at least into the fifth century by such notables as Irenaus, Clement of Alexandria, Justin Martyr, Athanasius, and Augustine.[11] We Latter-day Saints might not agree with some of what was taught about deification by such Christian thinkers, but it is clear that the idea was not foreign to the people of the early church.

Because all human beings, like Christ, are made in the image and likeness of God (Genesis 1:27; Moses 2:27), we feel it is neither audacity nor heresy for the children of God to aspire to be like him (Matthew 5:48; 1 John 3:2–3). Acquiring the attributes of godliness comes by overcoming the world through the Atonement (1 John 5:4–5; Revelation 2:7, 11; D&C 76:51–60), becoming heirs of God and joint-heirs with Christ, who is the natural Heir (Romans 8:17; Galatians 4:7), and thus inheriting all things, just as Jesus inherits all things (1 Corinthians 3:21–23; Revelation 21:7; D&C 76:55, 95; 84:38; 88:107). In that glorified state we will be conformed to the image of the Lord Jesus (Romans 8:29; 1 Corinthians 15:49; 2 Corinthians 3:18; 1 John 3:2; Alma 5:14), receive his glory, and be one with him and with the Father (John 17:21–23; Philippians 3:21).

Nor has the idea of the ultimate deification of man been completely lost from Christian thinking in our own time. "The Son of God became a man," C. S. Lewis pointed out, "to enable men to become sons of God."[12] Further, Lewis explained, God "said (in the Bible) that we were 'gods' and He is going to make good His words. If we let Him—for we can prevent Him, if we choose—He will make the feeblest and filthiest of us into a god or goddess, a dazzling, radiant, immortal creature, pulsating all through with such energy and joy and wisdom and love as we cannot now imagine, a bright stainless mirror which reflects back to God perfectly (though, of course, on a smaller scale) His own boundless power and delight and goodness. The process will be long and in parts very painful; but that is what we are in for. Nothing less. He meant what He said."[13] Because Lewis did not elaborate, we do not fully know what he meant (or what he understood or intended) by these statements, but we do know that the doctrine of the deification of man did not originate with Lewis nor with the Latter-day Saints; it is to be found throughout Christian history and within Orthodox Christian theology today.

Although as Latter-day Saints we certainly accept the teachings of Joseph Smith regarding man's becoming like God, we do not fully comprehend all that is entailed by such a bold declaration. Subsequent and even current Church leaders have said little concerning which of God's attributes are communicable and which are incommunicable. We believe that becoming like God is entailed in eternal life (D&C 132:19–20), but we do not believe we will ever, worlds without end, unseat God the Eternal Father or his Only Begotten Son, Jesus Christ; those holy beings are and forever will be the Gods we worship. Even though we believe in the ultimate deification of man, I do not know of any authoritative statement in Latter-day Saint literature that suggests we will ever worship any being other than the ones within the Godhead. Elder Parley P. Pratt, an early apostle, wrote one of the first theological treatises within Mormonism. In describing those who are glorified and attain eternal life, he stated: "The difference between Jesus Christ and another immortal and celestial man is this—the man is subordinate to Jesus Christ and does nothing in and of himself, but does all things in the name of Christ and by his authority, being of the same mind and ascribing all the glory to him and his Father."[14] We believe in "one God" in the sense that we love and serve one Godhead, one divine presidency, each of whom possesses all of the attributes of Godhood (Alma 11:44; D&C 20:28).

President Gordon B. Hinckley observed that "the whole design of the gospel is to lead us onward and upward to greater achievement, even, eventually, to godhood. This great possibility was enunciated by the Prophet Joseph Smith in the King Follett sermon and emphasized by President Lorenzo Snow. . . .

"Our enemies have criticized us for believing in this. Our reply is that this lofty concept in no way diminishes God the Eternal Father. He is the Almighty. He is the Creator and Governor of the universe. He is the greatest of all and will always be so. But just as any earthly father wishes for his sons and daughters every success in life, so I believe our Father in Heaven wishes for his children that they might approach him in stature and stand beside him resplendent in godly strength and wisdom."[15]

6. *If these deeper, non-biblical Latter-day Saint teachings about God (that he has a physical body, that he was once a man, that man may become like him) are so fundamental to Mormonism, why are they not taught in the Book of Mormon?*

The Book of Mormon is said to contain "the fulness of the gospel of Jesus Christ" (D&C 20:9). This does not mean that it contains the fulness of gospel doctrine or that it contains all of the doctrines within the faith. The Book of Mormon teaches the fulness of the gospel—the message of salvation in Christ—with simple plainness. The repetitive focus in the Book of Mormon is upon such principles as faith, repentance, baptism, the Holy Ghost, enduring to the end, the Atonement, bodily resurrection, and eternal judgment. Many of the more distinctive doctrines of Mormonism are found in the Doctrine and Covenants and Pearl of Great Price. The Book of Mormon is what it is and teaches what it teaches best—namely, the doctrine of Christ. Latter-day Saints would not expect all of the principles and doctrines of the faith to be set forth within the pages of the Book of Mormon any more than traditional Christians would expect all of the doc trines of salvation to be articulated within the four Gospels.

7. Doesn't the Book of Mormon teach that there is only one God and that he is a spirit?

A study of the Book of Mormon clearly reveals the doctrine of the Godhead as we teach and believe in it now, as a twenty-first century Church (2 Nephi 25:16, 23; 31:10–15; 32:9; Jacob 4:4–5; Alma 12:33–34; Helaman 5:10–11; 3 Nephi 18:19–20; Mormon 7:5; 9:27; Ether 4:15; Moroni 4:3; 7:22, 26–27). On the other hand, it is obvious that Christ is the main character of the book and that the Nephite-Jaredite record is intended to bear solemn witness of his divine Sonship. We are taught over and over how to recognize and acknowledge our sin and thus our need for forgiveness and regeneration; how to call upon the Father in the name of the Son by the power of the Holy Ghost; how to exercise a lively faith and gain the saving hope that comes only through the Atonement; in short, we are instructed repeatedly how to come unto Christ and be perfected in him. The Book of Mormon prophets also teach that there is only one God, meaning one Godhead or divine presidency (2 Nephi 31:21; Alma 11:44; Mormon 7:7). In a very real way, the Gods are infinitely more one than they are separate; they just happen to be distinct individuals and separate Gods. For much of the story, the

Nephites look to the Lord Jehovah, who is Jesus Christ, for salvation, meaning they understand the need to rely wholly upon his merits, mercy, and grace. Jehovah was then a spirit; he had not yet taken a physical body and been born in Bethlehem as Jesus of Nazareth. We believe, however, that God the Father, the ultimate object of our worship (2 Nephi 25:16; Jacob 4:4–5), is an embodied and exalted Man.

8. Why do the Latter-day Saints reject the traditional doctrine of the Trinity?

Over the years that followed the death and resurrection of the Lord, Christians sought earnestly to "contend for the faith which was once delivered unto the saints" (Jude 1:3). The epistles of Paul, Peter, Jude, and John suggest that the falling away of the first-century Christian Church was well under way by the close of the first century. With the deaths of the apostles and the loss of the priesthood, the divine institutional power to perform saving ordinances (sacraments), learn the mind of God, and interpret scripture was no longer on earth. To be sure, there were noble men and women throughout the earth during the centuries that followed, religious persons of goodwill, learned individuals who sought to hold the church together and to preserve holy writ. But a cardinal Latter-day Saint belief is that they acted without prophetic authority.

In an effort to satisfy Jews who denounced the notion of three Gods (Father, Son, and Holy Ghost) as polytheistic and at the same time to incorporate appealing Greek philosophical concepts of an all-powerful moving force in the universe, the Christian church began to redefine the Father, Son, and Holy Spirit. Religious historian Edwin Hatch described the intersection of Christian theology and Greek philosophy: "It is impossible for any one, whether he be a student of history or no, to fail to notice a difference of both form and content between the Sermon on the Mount and the Nicene Creed. . . . The one belongs to a world of Syrian peasants, the other to a world of Greek philosophers." He continued: "The religion which our Lord preached was rooted in Judaism. 'It came not to destroy, but to fulfil.' It took the Jewish conception of a Father in heaven, and gave it a new meaning. . . . In a similar way we shall find that the Greek Christianity of the fourth century was rooted in Hellenism. The Greek minds which had been ripening for Christianity had absorbed new ideas and new motives."[16]

The following are just some of the incorrect teachings adopted and adapted from Greek thought: a strict monotheism, a belief in only one God; an absolute distinction between mind and created things; God as utterly transcendent, existing outside time and space; the inferiority of created things; the incomprehensible and unknowable God; the incorporeality of God; and the notion that God is immutable, that he never changes.[17]

Over the centuries, debate on the nature of God, Christ, and the Holy Spirit took place at Nicaea (325), Constantinople (381), Ephesus (431), and Chalcedon (451), resulting in creedal statements that became the walk and talk of Christian doctrine. Men sought to harmonize revealed doctrine with Greek philosophy, which resulted in the costly alteration of fundamental truths. Roman Catholic scholar Father Charles Curran observed: "The older Catholic understanding used to talk about the scripture *and* the tradition. . . . [I]f you see tradition as accounts of the followers of the Holy Spirit to understand and appropriate the Gospel in the light of the changing culture and historical circumstances, then I think you have a very accurate description of the role of tradition in the church." He added: "For example, we went through the problem of appropriating the word in the fourth, fifth and sixth centuries with the great trinitarian and

Christological councils where we finally came to the conclusion of three persons in God and two natures in Jesus. Many people at the time said, 'Well, you can't say that because those words aren't in the scriptures.' That's right, they aren't in the scriptures, they are borrowed from Greek philosophy, but they are the on-going account of the believing community to understand, appropriate and live the word of God in its own circumstances."[18]

The noted anti-Christian writer of the second century, Celsus, stated: "The Christians say that God has hands, a mouth, and a voice; they are always proclaiming that 'God said this' or 'God spoke.' 'The heavens declare the work of his hands,' they say. I can only comment that such a God is no god at all, for *God has neither hands, mouth, nor voice, nor any characteristics of which we know.* And they say that God made man in his own image, failing to realize that God is not at all like a man, nor vice versa; *God resembles no form known to us.* . . . [W]e know that God is without shape, without color. They say that God moved above the waters he created—but *we know that it is contrary to the nature of God to move.* Their absurd doctrines even contain reference to God walking about in the garden he created for man; and they speak of him being angry, jealous, moved to repentance, sorry, sleepy—in short, as being in every respect more a man than a God. *They have not read Plato,* who teaches us in the *Republic* that God (the Good) does not even participate in being."[19]

One Evangelical Christian observed: "The classical theological tradition became misguided when, under the influence of Hellenistic philosophy, it defined God's perfection in static, time-less terms. All change was considered an imperfection and thus not applicable to God."[20] Further, "since Plato, Western philosophy has been infatuated with the idea of an unchanging, timeless reality. Time and all change were considered less real and less

good than the unchanging timeless realm. . . . This infatuation
with the 'unchanging' unfortunately crept into the church early
on and has colored the way Christians look at the world, read
their Bibles, and develop their theology."[21]

Such Platonic concepts concerning God as immutability (no
change), impassibility (no feelings or passions), and timelessness
made their way into Christian theology. As one group of
Christian scholars has stated: "Many Christians experience an
inconsistency between their beliefs about the nature of God and
their religious practice. For example, people who believe that
God cannot change his mind sometimes pray in ways that would
require God to do exactly that. And Christians who make use of
the free will defense for the problem of evil sometimes ask God
to get them a job or a spouse, or keep them from being harmed,
implying that God should override the free will of others in order
to achieve these ends. . . .

"These inharmonious elements are the result of the coupling
of biblical ideas about God with notions of the divine nature
drawn from Greek thought. The inevitable encounter between
biblical and classical thought in the early church generated many
significant insights and helped Christianity evangelize pagan
thought and culture. Along with the good, however, came a certain theological virus that infected the Christian doctrine of God,
making it ill and creating the sorts of problems mentioned above.
The virus so permeates Christian theology that some have come
to take the illness for granted, attributing it to divine mystery,
while others remain unaware of the infection altogether."[22]

Latter-day Saints believe that the simplest and clearest reading of the four Gospels sets forth a Godhead of three distinct
beings and three Gods—not three coequal persons in one substance or essence. Most traditional Christians, including many
scholars, freely admit that the doctrine of the Trinity is a mystery,

one that no mortal can comprehend and few can articulate. Jesus taught that it is life eternal to know God (John 17:3). As Christian scholar Millard Erickson has observed: "If God is infinite and we are finite, we will never be fully able to understand him. The fullness of what he is will exceed our powers to grasp. Thus, we cannot expect ever to resolve fully this great mystery."[23] Erickson acknowledged that although the Trinity is at the heart of most Christian theology, "this does not mean that complete and absolutely accurate understanding of the Trinity is essential for one to be a true Christian. *We are saved by our trust in Jesus Christ and in the Triune God, not by our subscription to correct theology.*"[24] Roman Catholic theologian Karl Rahner has pointed out, "We must be willing to admit that, should the doctrine of the Trinity have to be dropped as false, the major part of religious literature could well remain virtually unchanged." Further, "the Christian's idea of the incarnation would not have to change at all if there were no Trinity."[25]

CHAPTER 7

CHRIST AND SALVATION

One important religious issue in the world today is whether Latter-day Saints are Christians. Although the answer seems obvious to members of The Church of Jesus Christ of Latter-day Saints, it is not so obvious to those who might be called more "traditional Christians." The following questions are among those that often arise concerning our belief in Jesus of Nazareth, our relationship with him, and our commitment to him and his gospel.

1. *Haven't the Latter-day Saints attempted to change their public image over the last several years to emphasize their belief in Jesus Christ?*

Nothing in our doctrine of Christ has changed in the past 175 years. To some extent, however, there has been a change in emphasis by Church leaders, and that change may be reflected in the Church's public affairs efforts.

Suppose a very devout Baptist minister, the only one in his community, encountered stiff opposition from a man who simply disliked Baptists. Suppose the critic began a smear campaign with brochures, booklets, books, and videos that stated in no uncertain terms that Baptists were not only not Christian but atheists! The Baptist minister might initially smile at the ridiculous propaganda and dismiss it with a wave of the hand, concluding that no sane listener or viewer would give the anti-Baptist materials a moment's thought. But let's suggest further that after a decade of constant chants of "Baptists are not Christian!" and "Baptists are atheists!" a noticeable proportion of the public began to believe or at least attend to the propaganda. What should the Baptist minister do? Would it be inappropriate or beneath his dignity to begin a similar campaign to set the record straight? Not at all.

A critic might dismiss this example on the basis that the analogy does not hold because, he believes, Mormons really are not Christian. Such a statement gets me to my point. The problem with saying that Latter-day Saints are not Christian is that such a statement is in many ways untrue and is almost always misleading. Certainly there differences between the Latter-day Saint view of Jesus Christ and the traditional Christian view, but to say that we are not Christian is to lead some who know little of us to conclude that we are un-Christlike, anti-Christian, opposed to the teachings of Jesus, or rejecting of the message of the New Testament. The Church of Jesus Christ of Latter-day Saints has therefore begun to emphasize its heartfelt acceptance of Jesus as the Christ so that people in the world may not misunderstand the fundamental beliefs of the Church. We believe what is in the New Testament, and we believe what we feel God has revealed in the latter days concerning Christ. Such belief, such teachings, did not spring into existence within the last few years; they have been in the Book of Mormon, Doctrine and Covenants, Pearl of Great Price, and the teachings of Church leaders from the beginning, nearly two centuries ago.

Let me illustrate the challenge the Church faces. Several years ago a colleague and I were asked to participate in an interview with representatives of a Christian organization that was preparing a video presentation on The Church of Jesus Christ of

Latter-day Saints. My interview—which consisted of my responding to a series of questions—lasted for about an hour and a half. We covered much ground, including Latter-day Saint views of the role of prophets, the Bible, the person and nature of God the Father, and Jesus Christ. For twenty or thirty minutes, I described our understanding of the Atonement and of the necessity of the mercy and grace of Christ. When the video was released about a year later, I felt that it portrayed quite accurately, for the most part, our fundamental beliefs and, of course, the differences between Latter-day Saint and other Christian beliefs. One part was, however, particularly troublesome to me: the narrator stated quite emphatically that the Latter-day Saints do not believe in salvation by the grace of Christ.

A few months later, we met once again with representatives of this group. They were eager to know our feelings about the video. We commented that we appreciated the opportunity Latter-day Saints had been given to express themselves. At the same time, we expressed our disappointment in what had been said in the video about our lack of belief in grace. I said, essentially, "If you want to say that the Latter-day Saints have an *unusual* view of grace or a *different* view of grace, we can live with that, for we obviously have differences between our two faiths. But to say that we have *no* view of grace is a serious misrepresentation that confuses and misleads people."

When Ezra Taft Benson became the thirteenth president of the Church in 1985, he strongly emphasized the use of the Book of Mormon in the Church, stressing that the doctrines and teachings of the Book of Mormon are foundational and should be studied and discussed and applied more regularly by the Latter-day Saints. The Book of Mormon is grounded in redemptive theology, and the emphasis by Church leaders of its teachings over the past two decades have naturally resulted in a more Christ-centered emphasis in the whole Church.

President Gordon B. Hinckley remarked: "Those who observe us say that we are moving into the mainstream of religion. We are not changing. The world's perception of us is changing. We teach the same doctrine. We have the same organization. We labor to perform the same good works. But the old hatred is disappearing; the old persecution is dying. People are better informed. They are coming to realize what we stand for and what we do."[1]

2. Don't the Latter-day Saints believe that Jesus is literally the Son of God, through a physical relationship between God and Mary?

Latter-day Saints believe that Jesus is in reality the Only Begotten Son of God in the flesh. How that was accomplished we really do not know. Any efforts to go beyond the plain and straightforward statement that Jesus of Nazareth is the Son of God the Father is speculative and thus not a part of the doctrine of our Church.

3. Why do the Latter-day Saints not adorn themselves, their literature, or their homes or churches with crosses? Do they not believe in the saving efficacy of Jesus' death on the cross?

Latter-day Saints believe and teach that the Atonement of Jesus Christ is the central act of all history, just as do all other Christians around the world. Because Jesus was crucified, the cross has become for Latter-day Saints, as well as other Christians, associated with the Atonement (1 Corinthians 1:17–18; Galatians 6:12–14; Philippians 2:5–9; 3:18; Hebrews 12:2; 3 Nephi 12:30; Moses 7:55). According to Latter-day Saint teachings, however, Jesus' suffering in the Garden of Gethsemane was not just the awful anticipation of the cross.

Instead, we believe the atoning sacrifice was performed in the Garden of Gethsemane and also on the cross of Calvary. Christ's suffering and the shedding of his blood that began in Gethsemane was completed on Golgotha the next day, and then, in fulfillment of his redemptive mission, he rose from the tomb on the third day. Elder Gordon B. Hinckley noted that "for us, the cross is the symbol of the dying Christ, while our message is a declaration of the living Christ." He explained further that "the lives of our people must become the only meaningful expression of our faith and in fact, therefore, the symbol of our worship."[2]

Jesus needed to suffer and die to forgive our sins and thus deliver us from spiritual death. He also needed to rise from the dead, to offer the hope of resurrection by overcoming physical death. The risen Lord declared to the people of the Book of Mormon: "Behold I have given unto you my gospel, and this is the gospel which I have given unto you—that I came into the world to do the will of my Father, because my Father sent me. And *my Father sent me that I might be lifted up upon the cross;* and after that I had been lifted up upon the cross, that I might draw all men unto me, that as I have been lifted up by men even so should men be lifted up by the Father, to stand before me, to be judged of their works, whether they be good or whether they be evil" (3 Nephi 27:13–14; emphasis added). In that spirit, President Joseph F. Smith reminded us that "having been born anew, which is the putting away of the old man sin, and putting on of the man Christ Jesus, we have become soldiers of the Cross, having enlisted under the banner of Jehovah for time and for eternity."[3] Having accepted the atonement of Jesus Christ in our lives, we as Latter-day Saints strive to live so that others can see in us and our actions a living memorial to the living Christ.

4. Do the Latter-day Saints believe that they are saved by their own good works? Don't they believe in grace?

The plan of life and salvation is a covenant, a two-way promise between God and man. On his part, God has done for us what we could never do for ourselves. He created the earth and all things on it and in it. He opened the door for Adam and Eve to partake of the forbidden fruit and thereby introduce mortality, a time of testing but also a time of experience and opportunity. And, of course, he made available redemption from individual sins and renovation from a nature that is easily enticed by the world. The act of redemption is indeed the great act of love on the part of the Eternal Father. "For God so loved the world, that he gave his only begotten Son, that whosoever believeth in him should not perish, but have everlasting life" (John 3:16).

Like his Father, Jesus Christ has done for us what we could never do for ourselves. He suffered and bled and died for us. He redeemed us from sin. He offers to change our nature, to make us into new creatures, people bent on goodness. He rose from the dead and thereby opened the door for us to do the same thing at the appointed time. The gospel of Christ is "the power of God unto salvation" (Romans 1:16). The new life in Christ is not merely a cosmetic change, not just an alteration in behavior. It is in fact a new creation. Only Christ, who possesses the powers of a God, can do such things.

The scriptures are consistent in declaring that no unclean thing can enter into God's kingdom. In theory there are two ways by which we may become clean and thus inherit eternal life.

The first is simply to live the law of God perfectly, to make no mistakes. To do so is to be justified—pronounced innocent, declared blameless—by works or by law. To say this another way, if we keep the commandments completely (including receiving the sacraments, or ordinances, of salvation), never deviating from the strait and narrow path throughout our mortal lives, then we qualify for the blessings of the obedient. And yet we encounter on every side the terrible truth that all are unclean as a result of sin (Romans 3:23). All of us have broken at least one of the laws of God and therefore disqualify ourselves for justification by law or by works. Moral perfection may be a possibility, but it is certainly not a probability. Jesus alone trod that path. "Therefore," Paul observed, "by the deeds of the law"—meaning the law of Moses, as well as any law of God—"there shall no flesh be justified in his sight" (Romans 3:20; compare 2 Nephi 2:5).

The second way to be justified is by faith; it is for the sinner to be pronounced clean or innocent through trusting in and relying upon the merits of Him who answered the ends of the law (Romans 10:4; compare 2 Nephi 2:6–7), who did keep the law of God perfectly. Jesus owed no personal debt to justice. Because we are guilty of transgression, if there had been no atonement of Christ, no amount of good deeds on our part, no nobility independent of divine intercession, could make up for the loss. Truly, "since man had fallen he could not merit anything of himself" (Alma 22:14). Thus he who loved us first (1 John 4:10, 19) reaches out to the lost and fallen, to the disinherited, and proposes a marriage. The Infinite One joins with the finite, the Finished with the unfinished, the Whole with the partial, in short, the Perfect with the imperfect. Through covenant with Christ and thus union with the Bridegroom, we place ourselves in a condition to become fully formed, whole, finished—to become perfect in Christ (Moroni 10:32; D&C 76:69).

Latter-day Saints would be the first to acknowledge that though our own efforts to be righteous are necessary, those efforts will forevermore be insufficient. Paul teaches the profound truth that as we come unto Christ by the covenant of faith, our Lord's righteousness becomes our righteousness. The Savior justifies us in the sense that he *imputes* to us—meaning, he reckons to our account—his goodness and takes our sin. That is the great exchange. To the Corinthians Paul explained that "God was in Christ, reconciling the world unto himself, not imputing their trespasses unto them. . . . For *he* [God the Father] *hath made him* [Christ the Son] *to be sin for us,* who knew no sin; *that we might be made the righteousness of God in him*" (2 Corinthians 5:19, 21; emphasis added). As Paul explained elsewhere, Christ "hath redeemed us from the curse of the law, being made a curse for us" (Galatians 3:13; compare Hebrews 2:9).

From one Latter-day Saint writer's perspective, then, being justified is not only a matter of "acquittal" from guilt and sin but also of "being regarded as 'righteous' in a future Divine judgment."[4] Those who enter the gospel covenant, seek to do their duty, and endure to the end, the Lord holds "guiltless" (3 Nephi 27:16; compare D&C 4:2). It is not that they are guiltless in the sense of having never done wrong; rather, they are guiltless because the Holy One removes their blame and imputes to the repentant sinner, the one who comes unto Christ by covenant, His own righteousness. "For as by one man's disobedience"—the fall of Adam—"many were made sinners, so by the obedience of one"— Jesus Christ—"shall many be made righteous" (Romans 5:19).

Not one of us, of ourselves or on our own, is qualified to go where Christ is or to inherit what he has. But when we accept him as Lord and Savior by covenant, he treats us as though we had arrived. "A comparison may be made by reference to a man on an escalator. We anticipate that he will reach a given floor if he stays on the escalator. So a person will eventually be justified, but may be regarded as being so now, if he retains a remission of sins (Mosiah 4:26) and continually shows his faith in God."[5]

What, then, is expected of us? More is required than a verbal expression of faith, more than a confession with the lips that we have received Christ into our hearts. There is no question but that the power to save, to change, to renew is in Christ. There is no question but that only Christ can do this. But we, like the man on the escalator, must stay on the escalator ourselves—that is, stay in covenant. People who come unto Christ must have faith in Jesus Christ, repent of their sins, be baptized for the remission of sins, receive the gift of the Holy Ghost, and endure faithfully to the end of their days. Our good works are *necessary* to show our faith in Christ, but they are not *sufficient* for salvation. The theological debate between whether we are saved by grace or by works has continued for centuries. In reality, it is a meaningless argument that generates more heat than light. It is, in the words of C. S. Lewis, "like asking which blade in a pair of scissors is most necessary."[6]

"How else could salvation possibly come?" Elder Bruce R. McConkie asked. "Can man save himself? Can he resurrect himself? Can he create a celestial kingdom and decree his own admission thereto? Salvation must and does originate with God, and if man is to receive it, God must bestow it upon him, which bestowal is a manifestation of grace. . . .

". . . Salvation does not come by the works and performances of the law of Moses, nor by 'circumcision,' nor by 'the law of commandments contained in ordinances' . . . , nor does it come by any good works standing alone. No matter how righteous a man might be, no matter how great and extensive his good works, he could not save himself. Salvation is in Christ and comes through his atonement."[7]

As Elder Dallin H. Oaks has observed: "Man unquestionably has impressive powers and can bring to pass great things by tireless efforts and indomitable will. But after all our obedience and good works, we cannot be saved from the effect of our sins without the grace extended by the atonement of Jesus Christ."[8]

5. Do Latter-day Saints believe in being "born again?" Are they "saved"?

The doctrine of spiritual rebirth is as old as the world. Indeed, it was taught to Adam and Eve (Moses 6:58–60). The Nephite prophets declared over and over again that all of us need to be spiritually born of God, changed from our carnal and fallen state to a state of righteousness, having the image of Christ engraven in our countenances (Mosiah 27:24–26; Alma 5:14). In the meridian of time, Jesus repeated the commandment to be born again (John 3:3–5), and Joseph Smith taught that "the Son of God came into the world to redeem it from the fall. But except a man be born again, he cannot see the kingdom of God." Further, no one can inherit the highest heaven "unless he becomes as a little child, and is taught by the Spirit of God."[9]

Although the ultimate blessings of salvation do not come until the next life, in a sense people in this life may enjoy the assurance of salvation and the peace that accompanies that knowledge (D&C 59:23). True faith in Christ produces hope in Christ—not worldly wishing but expectation, anticipation, assurance. As the apostle Paul wrote, the Holy Spirit provides the "earnest of our inheritance" (Ephesians 1:14), the promise or evidence that we are on course, in covenant, and thus in line for full salvation in the world to come (2 Corinthians 1:21–22; 5:5). That is, the Spirit of God operating in our lives is like the Lord's "earnest money" on us—his sweet certification that he seriously intends to save us with an everlasting salvation. Thus, if we are striving to cultivate the gift of the Holy Ghost, we are living in what might be called a "saved" condition.

A highly respected Evangelical theologian, John Stott, has

written: "Salvation is a big and comprehensive word. It embraces the totality of God's saving work, from beginning to end. In fact, salvation has three tenses, past, present, and future. . . . 'I have been saved (in the past) from the penalty of sin by a crucified Saviour. I am being saved (in the present) from the power of sin by a living Saviour. And I shall be saved (in the future) from the very presence of sin by a coming Saviour' . . .

"If therefore you were to ask me, 'Are you saved?' there is only one correct biblical answer which I could give you: 'yes and no.' Yes, in the sense that by the sheer grace and mercy of God through the death of Jesus Christ my Saviour he has forgiven my sins, justified me and reconciled me to himself. But no, in the sense that I still have a fallen nature and live in a fallen world and have a corruptible body, and I am longing for my salvation to be brought to its triumphant completion."[10]

President Brigham Young taught: "It is present salvation and the present influence of the Holy Ghost that we need every day to keep us on saving ground. . . .

"I want present salvation. I preach, comparatively, but little about the eternities and Gods, and their wonderful works in eternity; and do not tell who first made them, nor how they were made; for I know nothing about that. *Life is for us, and it is for us to receive it today,* and not wait for the millennium. Let us take a course to be saved today, and, when evening comes, review the acts of the day, repent of our sins, if we have any to repent of, and say our prayers; then we can lie down and sleep in peace until the morning, arise with gratitude to God, commence the labours of another day, and strive to live the whole day to God and nobody else."[11]

"I am in the hands of the Lord," President Young pointed out, "and never trouble myself about my salvation, or what the Lord will do with me hereafter."[12] As he said on another occasion, "our work is a work of the present. The salvation we are seeking is for the present, and, sought correctly, it can be obtained, and be continually enjoyed. If it continues to-day, it is upon the same principle that it will continue to-morrow, the next day, the next week, or the next year, and, we might say, the next eternity."[13]

President David O. McKay likewise explained that "the gospel of Jesus Christ, as revealed to the Prophet Joseph Smith, is in very deed, in every way, the power of God unto salvation. It is salvation *here*—here and now. It gives to every man the perfect life, here and now, as well as hereafter."[14] He also taught: "Sometimes we think of salvation as a state of bliss after we die. I should like to think of salvation as a condition here in life today. I like to think that my Church makes me a better man, my wife a better woman, a sweeter wife, my children nobler sons and daughters, here and now. . . .

"I look upon the Gospel as a power contributing to those conditions."[15]

In short, salvation is in Christ, and our covenant with Christ, our trust in his power to redeem us, should be demonstrated in how we live. The influence of the Holy Ghost in our lives is a sign to us that we are on course, "in Christ" (2 Corinthians 5:17), and thus in line for salvation.

6. *If the Latter-day Saints really do believe that salvation comes through Christ, why do they build temples and participate in temple ordinances?*

President Gordon B. Hinckley taught that "each temple built by The Church of Jesus Christ of Latter-day Saints stands as an expression of the testimony of this people that God our Eternal Father lives, that He has a plan for the blessing of His sons and daughters of all generations, that His Beloved Son, Jesus the Christ, who was born in Bethlehem of Judea and crucified on the cross of Golgotha, is the Savior and Redeemer of the world, whose atoning sacrifice makes possible the fulfillment of that plan in the eternal life of each who accepts and lives the gospel." "These unique and wonderful buildings," he stated on another occasion, "and the ordinances administered therein, represent the ultimate in our worship. These ordinances become the most profound expressions of our theology." Thus the temple is "a statement that we as a people believe in the immortality of the human soul. . . . It speaks of life here and life beyond the grave."[16]

We believe, as do most Christians, that the ancient tabernacle and temples were types of the Savior. That is, the "placement, the furniture, the clothing—each item was specified by the Lord to bear witness, in typology, symbolism and similitude of Jesus Christ and his atoning sacrifice."[17] This appears to be the message of Hebrews 9 and 10. "Accordingly," Brother Tad R. Callister has observed, "it should not seem surprising that the Atonement is a focal point of modern temple worship, just as it was in ancient times."[18] We believe the temple and its ordinances to be the highest channel of grace, indeed, the culminating channel, the means by which men and women are endowed with power from on high (Luke 24:49). These ordinances serve as extensions and reminders of the Lord's infinite and eternal Atonement. As Truman G. Madsen has pointed out, "The rebirth that climaxes all rebirths is in the House of the Lord."[19]

The covenants and ordinances of the temple, wrote Elder James E. Talmage, "embody certain obligations on the part of the individual," such that he or she promises "to observe the law of strict virtue and chastity, to be charitable, benevolent, tolerant and pure; to devote both talent and material means to the spread of truth and the uplifting of the race; to maintain devotion to the cause of truth; and to seek in every way to contribute to the great preparation that the earth may be made ready to receive her King,—the Lord Jesus Christ."[20] As Brother Callister has written, "An integral part of the temple experience is the making of covenants. Why? Because faithful observance of those covenants can help to bring about the broken heart and contrite spirit that allow us to more fully enjoy the infinite blessings of the Atonement." Further, "It is our privilege, in the sanctity of these holy places, to commune and reflect more meaningfully upon the Savior and his vicarious act of love for each of us, and then to receive of that endowing power that lifts us heavenward." In short, "the Atonement is the focal point of each saving ordinance."[21]

Because for Latter-day Saints the ordinances or sacraments are essential—inasmuch as they represent, symbolize, and epitomize our covenants with Christ—we believe that each son and daughter of God must receive the sacraments to gain the highest of eternal rewards. We believe, further, that if the opportunity to receive such rites is not possible in mortality, it will be made available in the world to come. Thus temples become the place of covenant, the place of ordinance, for both the living and the dead. A living person may thus enter the temple and be baptized, for example, in behalf of one who has died. "This is a sanctuary of service," President Hinckley pointed out. "Most of the work done in this sacred house is performed vicariously in behalf of those who have passed beyond the veil of death. I know of no other work to compare with it. It more nearly approaches the vicarious sacrifice of the Son of God in behalf of all mankind than any other work of which I am aware. . . . It is a service of the living in behalf of the dead. It is a service which is of the very essence of selflessness."[22]

Elder Marion D. Hanks explained, "As the mission of the Church is to 'invite all to come unto Christ,' so I believe, in its clearest and loveliest sense, that this is *also the mission of temples,* where we not only undertake the sacred service of work for redemption of the dead, to open the door for them, but where the choicest of all opportunities exists to learn of Christ, and to come to know him and commune with him and to purify our own hearts."[23]

While Latter-day Saints believe and teach that the highest form of salvation, or exaltation, comes to those who receive the blessings of the temple (D&C 131:1–4), we do not in any way believe that it is the temple, or the ordinances contained there, that save us. Salvation is in Christ. We believe the temple to be a house of learning, of communion and inspiration, of covenants and ordinances, of service, and of personal refinement. We believe that the temple is the house of the Lord. But it is not the Lord. We look to Christ the Person for salvation.

7. Isn't it true that Latter-day Saints belong to a cult?

The derisive label *cult* frightens many people, conjuring up images of the bizarre, the unnatural, and even the demonic. And yet the first two definitions of *cult* in *Merriam-Webster's Eleventh Collegiate Dictionary* are synonymous with *religion.* The third definition is the one, I suppose, most anti-Mormons have in mind: "a religion regarded as an unorthodox or spurious sect." One writer described cults as follows: they are started by strong and dynamic leaders; they believe in additional scripture; they have rigid standards for membership; they proselyte new converts; the leaders or officials of the cult are not professional clergymen; they believe in ongoing and continual communication from God; and they claim some truth not available to other individuals or groups.[24] By these standards, of course, the Latter-day Saints would certainly qualify as a cult. Of course, so would the New Testament Christian Church!

8. Are the Latter-day Saints Christian? Or do they, as many believe, worship a "different Jesus"?

Latter-day Saints accept and endorse the testimony of the New Testament writers. Jesus is the Promised Messiah, the Resurrection and the Life (John 11:25), the Light of the world (John 8:12). Everything that testifies of his divine birth, his goodness, his transforming power, and his godhood, we embrace enthusiastically. But we also rejoice in the additional knowledge latter-day prophets have provided about our Lord and Savior.

Latter-day Saints proclaim that Jesus of Nazareth is the Christ. We have taken his name upon us, eagerly acknowledge the redeeming power of his blood and the reality of his resurrection from the dead, and seek to emulate his perfect life. To paraphrase the apostle Paul, the Spirit bears witness with our spirits (Romans 8:16) that Jesus is the Christ, the Son of the Living God, and that he was crucified for the sins of the world. Knowing what we know, feeling what we feel, and having experienced what we have in regard to the person and power of the Savior, it is sometimes difficult for us to be patient with those who denounce us as non-Christian or cultists. But we are constrained to do so in the spirit of Him who also was misunderstood and misrepresented. Although it would be a wonderful thing to have others acknowledge our Christianity, we do not court their favor nor will we compromise our distinctiveness to gain acceptance or popularity.

9. Isn't the Latter-day Saint claim to be "the only true church" exclusionary and unchristian?

Latter-day Saints believe that truth is to be found throughout the earth—among peoples in all walks of life, among sages and philosophers, and among persons of differing religious persuasions. But we also claim that through the call of Joseph Smith and his successors and through the establishment of The Church of Jesus Christ of Latter-day Saints, the *fulness* of the gospel of Jesus Christ has been restored to earth. We value the truths had among the children of God everywhere, but we believe that ours is the "only true church" in the sense that the same divine authority and the same doctrines of salvation had from the beginning are now to be found *in their fulness* in the Latter-day Saint faith.

10. Why do Latter-day Saints send missionaries throughout the world, especially to those who are already Christian?

Before The Church of Jesus Christ of Latter-day Saints was even organized, a spirit of enthusiasm and zeal was evident among those who received the message of Joseph Smith and the Book of Mormon that God had chosen to restore truths and authority to earth. That spirit intensified after the formal organization of the Church. Many of the revelations recorded in the Doctrine and Covenants instruct the Latter-day Saints to travel, to preach, and to bear witness. The Saints are told to proclaim the message of the Restoration before individuals and congregations, in churches and in synagogues. Because we believe that what we have to share with others is a fulness of the gospel of Jesus Christ and that fulness is not found elsewhere, we feel a responsibility to make the message available to all who will hear. The commission given to the apostles when Jesus ascended into heaven, a commission to make disciples of all nations (Matthew 28:19–20; Mark 16:15–18), has been repeated and renewed to the Latter-day Saints: "Go ye into all the world, preach the gospel to every creature, acting in the authority which I have given you, baptizing in the name of the Father, and of the Son, and of the Holy Ghost (D&C 68:8).

As Church president George Albert Smith said to those not

of the Latter-day Saint faith: "We have come not to take away from you the truth and virtue you possess. We have come not to find fault with you nor to criticize you. We have not come here to berate you because of things you have not done; but we have come here as your brethren . . . and to say to you: 'Keep all the good that you have, and let us bring to you more good, in order that you may be happier and in order that you may be prepared to enter into the presence of our Heavenly Father.'"[25]

Those who are content with what they have are perfectly free to say so to our members or full-time missionaries. Those who are curious, who may be unsatisfied with their present faith or way of life, or who may be seeking for answers to some of life's puzzling questions, may find an encounter with the Latter-day Saints worth their time and attention.

CHAPTER 8

JOSEPH SMITH AND CHURCH HISTORY

The psalmist spoke prophetically of the last days: When the wicked "bend their bow; lo, they make ready their arrow upon the string, that they may privily shoot at the upright in heart, to destroy their foundation" (JST Psalm 11:2). Many of the questions raised by both interested investigators and zealous critics of the Church pertain to foundational events, to matters associated with the call and work of Joseph Smith, as well as to the ongoing work of the Restoration since the time of the First Vision. It is natural that questions should arise about the Choice Seer and the work he set in motion.

1. Why would God need to call a prophet such as Joseph Smith? Isn't the Bible the "end of the prophets"?

Latter-day Saints believe that it has been the pattern and practice of the Almighty to speak through his prophets, or covenant spokesmen, from the beginning of time. The Old Testament prophet Amos taught, "Surely the Lord God will do nothing, but he revealeth his secret unto his servants the prophets" (Amos 3:7). Although periods of apostasy, or falling away, have occurred through the ages, God has chosen repeatedly to restore divine truth through the calling of new prophets. Noah's instructions about building the ark were not sufficient for Abraham to understand the sacred covenant that God desired to make with him. Nor did Jehovah's instructions to Abraham make known the Ten Commandments on Sinai; God needed to raise up a Moses. The calling of prophets reached its apex with the coming into mortality of Jesus Christ, the great High Priest of our profession, our Lord and Redeemer.

After the Savior's death and the subsequent deaths of his apostles (those who had been given the keys of the kingdom of God), good men and women throughout the earth sought for centuries to keep the light of Christianity alive. There were evils and perversions and attacks on scripture and on the truth, to be sure, but remnants of the fulness of the gospel, relics of ancient Christianity, remained on the earth as the centuries passed. Great souls, such as the reformers, sought to rectify the misdeeds and doctrinal errors of the mother church and to make the scriptures more readily available to ordinary people. But a reformation was not sufficient. Divine authority and many plain and precious truths had been lost. A restoration was required.

Why shouldn't God call a prophet in the last days? Is the Bible really sufficient? Does the Bible itself suggest that there will never again be revelation and vision and prophecy through God's chosen servants? Does God love the people of our day any less than he loved those to whom he manifested himself in Old and New Testament times? Do we need the current and ongoing word of God any less today than did our forbears?

In truth, there never has been a day or a time in the history of the world in which the word of God was more sorely needed than it is today. The call of Joseph Smith as a modern prophet was no different from the call of ancient prophets, and, sadly, he is rejected for many of the same reasons his prophetic predecessors were rejected. The great question facing the religious world today and in the future is simply this: Was Joseph Smith called of God?

2. Do the Latter-day Saints worship Joseph Smith? What is the relationship between Joseph Smith and subsequent Church presidents?

The Latter-day Saints do not worship Joseph Smith any more than the people who lived some two thousand years before Jesus worshipped Abraham. Former-day Saints and Latter-day Saints do not worship prophets; rather they worship the Father in the name of the Son by the power of the Holy Ghost. We revere and respect, admire and sustain the apostles and prophets of our dispensation, but our worship is reserved for God.

All of the presidents of the Church who have succeeded Joseph Smith have held the same divine calling, the same priesthood authority, and have borne the designation of prophet, seer, and revelator to the Church. Joseph Smith is in a significant position in being a *dispensation head,* a man called to restore the knowledge of God, of Christ, and of the plan of salvation after a period of falling away. The dispensation head, a kind of prophet's prophet, is called to be the preeminent prophetic revealer of Christ. His task is to establish Christ's doctrines and authority once again on earth. Those who follow him in the prophetic office stand as echoes and affirmations of his original testimony to the world, and they also seek for and declare new revelation as it is needed.

3. Aren't there differences in detail between the varying accounts of Joseph Smith's First Vision?

There are several accounts of Joseph Smith's first vision, four of which were dictated by him. These four accounts were recorded in 1832, 1835, 1838 (the canonized account contained in the Pearl of Great Price), and 1842 (from the Wentworth Letter). The few differences between the accounts are minute and in most cases reflect a variation in tone or intent dependent upon the audience.

Church historian Richard Lloyd Anderson observed: "Criticisms of Joseph Smith demand consistency in studying the prophets. Many Christians accepting Paul comfortably think that their sniping at Joseph Smith's first vision has proved it wrong. But what appears is a double standard for these critics. Most arguments against Joseph Smith's first vision detract from Paul's Damascus experience with equal force. For instance, Joseph's credibility is attacked because he did not describe his first vision until a dozen years after it happened. But the first known mention of the Damascus appearance is in 1 Corinthians 9:1, written about two dozen years after it happened. Critics love to dwell on supposed inconsistencies in Joseph Smith's spontaneous accounts of his first vision. But people normally give shorter and longer accounts of a vivid experience that is retold more than once. Joseph Smith was cautious about public explanations of his sacred experiences until the Church grew strong and could properly publicize what God had given him. Thus his most detailed first-vision account came after several others—at the time that he began his formal history that he saw as one of the key responsibilities of his life (*see* JS–H 1:1–2, 17–20). In Paul's case there is the parallel. His most detailed account of Christ's call is the last recorded mention of several. Thus before Agrippa, Paul related how the glorified Savior first prophesied his work among the gentiles; this was told only then because Paul was speaking before a gentile audience (*see* Acts 26:16–18). Paul and Joseph Smith had reasons for delaying full details of their visions until the proper time and place."[1]

It seems reasonable that a person bent upon denying the reality of the First Vision because of differing details in the varying accounts would also be eager to deny the resurrection of

Jesus Christ on the basis that the Gospel writers could not agree on whether there was one angel or two at the Garden Tomb that first Easter morning. "The important thing," notes Elder Neal A. Maxwell, "is that the tomb was empty, because Jesus had been resurrected! Essence, not tactical detail!"[2]

4. Many Christians insist on a "priesthood of all believers." Why do Latter-day Saints teach of the need for specific priesthood authority?

The New Testament clearly teaches the need for divine authority. Jesus ordained the Twelve Apostles (John 15:16), gave them the keys of the kingdom of God (Matthew 16:18–19; 18:18), and empowered his servants to perform miracles and take the gospel to all nations (Matthew 10:1, 5–8; 28:19–20). Later, after the Lord's death, the apostles commissioned others to serve in the ministry (Acts 6:1–6; 13:1–3; 14:23; 1 Timothy 4:14; 2 Timothy 1:6; Titus 1:5) and to ensure that the saving ordinances or sacraments were performed only by those properly ordained (Acts 19:1–6, 13–16). This authority was a power that no one could assume, take upon himself, or purchase; it came only through the laying on of hands by those holding proper authority (Acts 8:18–20; Hebrews 5:4).

Within a hundred years of the crucifixion of Jesus and the deaths of the apostles, the authority or power to act in the name of God was lost from the earth. Centuries later noble and good men and women tried to reform the church during the era we know as the Protestant Reformation, but such persons acted without divine authority. According to historian John Callender, Roger Williams, the man known as the founder of the Baptist faith, "'renounced these opinions [the views of the Baptists], likewise, and turned seeker, i.e. to wait for new apostles to restore Christianity.'" He felt the need "'of a special commission, to restore the modes of positive worship, according to the original institution.'" Williams concluded, according to John Winthrop, "that the Protestants were 'not . . . able to derive the authority . . . from the apostles, . . . [but] conceived God would raise up some apostolic power.'"[3]

5. What is the Latter-day Saint doctrine of marriage?

The Church of Jesus Christ of Latter-day Saints teaches that marriage is more than a civil ordinance. It is, first and foremost, an institution, even a covenant, ordained of God. Marriage between one man and one woman is sacred. Because we as Latter-day Saints believe that marriage and the family were intended to survive death, to last forever, we teach that marriages performed in temples, by the proper authority, do not end with the death of the marriage partners but endure for time and all eternity.

6. Why did Joseph Smith and other early Latter-day Saints practice plural marriage?

The practice of plural marriage was introduced by the Prophet Joseph Smith on a very restricted basis while he was president of the Church (1830–44), and the principle was first announced publicly in a general conference of the Church in April 1852 during the presidency of Brigham Young. For more than fifty years, the Saints practiced plural marriage because God had commanded them to do so. Plural marriage was a religious principle, and that is the only reason the practice was maintained through decades of opposition and persecution.

Latter-day Saints believe that the practice of plural marriage was a part of the "restitution of all things" (Acts 3:21; D&C 132:40, 45), the grand plan of restoration by which principles, doctrines, covenants, and ordinances (sacraments) from ancient times were restored to earth. Church leaders have pointed out that monogamy is the rule and polygamy the exception; the unauthorized practice of plural marriage is condemned in the Book of Mormon (Jacob 2:23–30, 34; 3:5), the Doctrine and Covenants (132:38–39), the sermons of Joseph Smith himself,[4] and the teachings of current Church leaders.

Almost all who became Latter-day Saints during the nineteenth century had been associated with other religious societies before their conversion and had been reared in traditional, monogamous homes. The idea of a man having more than one wife contrasted sharply with all they had been brought up to believe. Therefore plural marriage was at first extremely difficult for many of the Saints to accept, including Joseph Smith, Brigham Young, and John Taylor. Elder Taylor remarked that "when this system was first introduced among this people, it was one of the greatest crosses that ever was taken up by any set of men since the world stood."[5] President Brigham Young declared: "I was not desirous of shrinking from any duty, nor of failing in the least to do as I was commanded, but it was the first time in my life that I had desired the grave, and I could hardly get over it for a long time. When I saw a funeral I felt to envy the corpse its situation and to regret that I was not in the coffin."[6]

Yet Latter-day Saints believe that whatever God commands is right and that plural marriages, when performed by the proper authority, were both legal and acceptable to God at that time. Men and women were expected to demonstrate loyalty and devotion to their spouse and to observe the highest standards of fidelity and morality, whether in monogamous marriage or in plural marriage.

There is scriptural precedent for the practice of authorized plural marriage, as illustrated in the lives of noble and faithful men and women in the Old Testament. For example, Abraham,

Jacob, and Moses married additional wives (Genesis 16:1–11; 29:28; 30:4, 9, 26; Exodus 2:21; Numbers 12:1), and there is no indication that God disapproved of their actions in any way. Nonetheless, God did condemn King David's unauthorized relationship with Bathsheba (2 Samuel 11–12) and King Solomon's marriages to foreign women, who turned his heart away from the worship of Jehovah (1 Kings 11). Further, evidence suggests that authorized plural marriages took place in the days of Jesus.[7] It was as a result of Joseph Smith's inquiry to God in the early 1830s about why plural marriage was practiced anciently that the divine instruction came to institute the practice in modern times.

Those who entered into this order of matrimony did so under the direction of the presiding authorities of the Church. Elder Orson Pratt, one of the early Latter-day Saint apostles who was at first opposed to the principle, stated later: "How are these things to be conducted? Are they to be left at random? Is every servant of God at liberty to run here and there, seeking out the daughters of men as wives unto themselves without any restrictions, law, or condition? No. We find these things were restricted in ancient times. Do you not recollect the circumstance of the Prophet Nathan's coming to David? He came to reprove him for certain disobedience. . . . Nathan the Prophet, in relation to David, was the man that held the keys concerning this matter in ancient days; and it was governed by the strictest laws.

"So in these last days; . . . there is but one man in all the world, at the same time, who can hold the keys of this matter; but one man has power to turn the key to inquire of the Lord, and to say whether I, or these my brethren, or any of the rest of this congregation, or the Saints upon the face of the whole earth, may have this blessing of Abraham conferred upon them; he holds the keys of these matters now, the same as Nathan, in his day."[8]

In the nineteenth century, when faced with a national anti-polygamy campaign, many Latter-day Saint women startled their eastern sisters (who had equated plural marriage with the oppression of women) by publicly demonstrating in favor of their right to live plural marriage as a religious principle. In January 1870 thousands of women met in the Salt Lake Tabernacle in what they called the "Great Indignation Meeting" to manifest their indignation and protest against anti-polygamy laws.

Public opposition in the United States to the practice of plural marriage grew during the last quarter of the nineteenth century. A number of Church officials were incarcerated, including George Q. Cannon, a member of the First Presidency. The government threatened to confiscate Church property, including the temples. In the wake of oppressive laws enacted by the Congress, Church president Wilford Woodruff sought the Lord in prayer on behalf of the Saints who were suffering individually and as a people. By revelation, the Lord withdrew the command to practice plural marriage. Church president Wilford Woodruff issued what has come to be known as the Manifesto, and a constituent assembly of the Latter-day Saints in general conference accepted it in October 1890. The Manifesto brought about a noticeable change in the public's attitude toward the Church. Since that time, the official doctrine and practice of the Church has been monogamous marriage between one man and one woman.

Various groups have broken away from The Church of Jesus Christ of Latter-day Saints over the practice of plural marriage. President Gordon B. Hinckley declared: "I wish to state categorically that this Church has nothing whatever to do with those practicing polygamy. They are not members of this Church. Most of them have never been members. . . .

"If any of our members are found to be practicing plural

marriage, they are excommunicated, the most serious penalty the Church can impose. . . .

"More than a century ago God clearly revealed unto His prophet Wilford Woodruff that the practice of plural marriage should be discontinued, which means that it is now against the law of God."[9]

As Latter-day Saints we believe in "obeying, honoring, and sustaining the law" (Article of Faith 12), so although we stand firmly against the practice of plural marriage today, we leave to local magistrates the enforcement of the civil law. Speaking of those who continue the practice, President Hinckley has said: "They are in violation of the civil law. They know they are in violation of the law. They are subject to its penalties. The Church, of course, has no jurisdiction whatever in this matter."[10]

7. What is the relationship between The Church of Jesus Christ of Latter-day Saints and the Reorganized Church of Jesus Christ of Latter Day Saints (now Community of Christ)?

After the death of Joseph Smith Jr., many wondered who should lead the Church. One group of Saints felt that the Prophet had given strict instructions that at his death the First Presidency would be dissolved and the Quorum of the Twelve Apostles, then under the direction of Brigham Young, would lead the people. Another group believed that Joseph the Prophet had ordained his eldest son to succeed him. The first group was led by Brigham Young from Nauvoo, Illinois, in 1846 and traveled across the plains to Salt Lake City. This group, sometimes called the "Utah Mormons" or the "Utah Church," was The Church of Jesus Christ of Latter-day Saints. In 1860 the second group formally organized themselves with Joseph Smith III as their leader. Their headquarters was moved from Plano, Illinois, to Lamoni, Iowa, and finally to Independence, Missouri. This was the Reorganized Church of Jesus Christ of Latter Day Saints (RLDS), known today as the Community of Christ. The first major division, therefore, between the two groups was over the question of succession—apostolic or patriarchal. Since 1860 the Latter-day Saints and Community of Christ have been divided over several matters of doctrine and practice.

8. *Is it true that the death penalty by firing squad still exists in the state of Utah because of a doctrine of "blood atonement" held by the Latter-day Saints?*

The Saints had settled in the Great Basin and struggled for a decade to survive. By 1856 it seemed to the leaders of the Church that spiritual discipline, which had been allowed to slip somewhat during the years of settlement, needed to be shored up. For the next year or so, the Saints underwent a revival in what has come to be known as the Mormon Reformation. Individuals and families were encouraged strongly to observe with exactness the standards of the faith and to return to the obedience they had demonstrated before the exodus. Sermons delivered by Church leaders clearly intended to strike fear into the hearts of the members—both condemning their sins and warning them of the dreadful consequences of sin. Like Jonathan Edwards's sermons about sinners in the hands of an angry God, many of these Latter-day Saint sermons were more revival rhetoric than statements of doctrine or practice.

The Church of Jesus Christ of Latter-day Saints has no official position on the death penalty for capital crimes. The only blood atonement that has saving value is the blood Atonement of Jesus Christ. Whether a state should impose the death penalty or how that penalty is to be carried out is not a Church matter; such decisions rest with the civil authorities.

9. *If the Latter-day Saints are a peaceful and peace-loving people,
how can they justify the Mountain Meadows Massacre?*

Many students of history have felt that the fiery sermons of
the Mormon Reformation contributed unwittingly to a growing
anxiety, tension, and fear among the Saints. The Mountain
Meadows Massacre of 1857 is truly one of the black marks on
our history, an event that has spawned ill will, guilt, and embarrassment for a century and a half. Factors that contributed to the
massacre of a wagon train of emigrants from Arkansas and
Missouri included the following: Johnston's Army had been dis-
patched to Utah, and a "Utah War" seemed inevitable; Elder
Parley P. Pratt had recently been brutally assassinated in Arkansas;
some who accompanied the Arkansan wagon train through Utah
Territory were Missourians who claimed to have participated in
the Haun's Mill Massacre in Missouri in which several Latter-day
Saints had been killed; and somewhat incendiary sermons of
Church leaders about those outside the faith who were seeking
to disturb the peace. In other words, there was in the air a tension, a stress, a war hysteria that hung over the people—Mormon
and non-Mormon alike.

As a result of these and perhaps other factors that incited the
local Church leaders and settlers to react, 120 people died in the
massacre at Mountain Meadows. There may have been reasons
why the Latter-day Saints chose to act as they did, but in reality
there is no excuse for what took place. It was an atrocity, both
uncivilized and unchristian. The Saints knew better and had been
taught to abide by a higher standard. There is no evidence that
President Brigham Young (who was in Salt Lake City) was in any
way responsible for what took place. He had, in fact, strongly
counseled the Saints in Southern Utah to allow the Arkansans to
make their way through the territory without hindrance.

10. How can the Latter-day Saints believe themselves to be the true church when they have changed so many beliefs and practices over the years?

The Church of Jesus Christ of Latter-day Saints is identified by revelation as the "only true and living church upon the face of the whole earth" (D&C 1:30). This truth in no way denies the truth and light to be found in other churches, religious groups, and individuals all across the globe, but it emphasizes that the fulness of the gospel and the power to act in the name of God are vested in the restored Church. It is true. It is living. "When the word *living* is used," Elder Neal A. Maxwell has written, "it carries a divinely deliberate connotation. The Church is neither dead nor dying, nor is it even wounded. The Church, like the living God who established it, is alive, aware, and functioning. It is not a museum that houses a fossilized faith; rather, it is a kinetic kingdom characterized by living faith in living disciples."[12]

As Elder Maxwell has intimated, our place as the true and living Church is inextricably linked to our belief in a true and living God, an Almighty Being who is dynamic and responsive, who attends to the current and pressing needs of his people. Our God is neither a static Supreme Being nor a distant Deity. He is neither unreachable nor unknowable. Like his Beloved Son, he is "touched with the feeling of our infirmities" (Hebrews 4:15).

Because he is a living God, our Heavenly Father is forevermore involved in the matter of change. While absolute truths and divinely revealed doctrines remain intact, forming the solid and secure foundation upon which we build, "the principle on which the government of heaven is conducted [is] revelation adapted to the circumstances in which the children of the kingdom are placed."[13] The living God reveals himself to those called and ordained as living prophets, whose ministry it is to stand as watchmen on the tower, to behold "things which [are] not visible to the natural eye," to perceive impending danger "afar off" (Moses 6:27, 36; compare D&C 101:45, 54). God changed his mind about destroying the city of Nineveh (Jonah 1–4); rescinded his word on the impending death of Hezekiah and added fifteen years to the king's life (Isaiah 38:1–5); and altered his policy concerning the gospel being taken solely to the house of Israel in the meridian of time (Matthew 10:5–6; 15:24; Acts 10). Thank God for prophets. Thank God for change.

11. Isn't it true that some of the prophecies of Joseph Smith and other Church leaders did not come to pass? Doesn't that invalidate their claim to divine authority?

Some prophecies are unconditional in nature; they will come to pass, despite the righteousness or wickedness of the people or the circumstances that arise. Lehi prophesied that the Messiah would come to earth six hundred years from the time his colony left Jerusalem (1 Nephi 10:4; 19:8; 2 Nephi 25:19). Many other prophets spoke of the teachings, sufferings, atonement, death, and resurrection of the Lord, and they did so in affirmative, straightforward terms, no strings attached. Indeed, the specific time of the second coming of the Son of Man is set and fixed; the world may choose to repent and become more and more righteous or drift into spiritual indifference and callous insensitivity for things spiritual—and it will not matter. The Lord will come at a certain time, a time that can neither be hurried nor delayed.[14]

Other prophecies and promises are conditional: They depend upon outward circumstances. Perhaps the best illustration of conditional prophetic promises is patriarchal blessings: the promises in them depend completely upon the faithfulness of the recipient. Such is also the case with the consummate promises of temple ordinances: they are conditional. In a revelation given through the Prophet Joseph Smith in September 1832, the Lord said that the temple in Independence, Jackson County, Missouri, would "be reared in this generation. For verily this generation shall not all pass away until an house shall be built unto the Lord, and a cloud shall rest upon it, which cloud shall be even the glory of the Lord, which shall fill the house" (D&C 84:4–5).

As we know, the Saints were driven from Independence in the summer of 1833 and eventually out of the state. A temple was not built. The glory of God, manifest in the divine Shekinah, or holy cloud, did not rest upon the edifice. We might point out that the word *generation,* as used in the prophecy, referred not to a period of thirty or forty years but rather to a dispensation. That may be what was meant, for example, when the Lord, speaking to Joseph Smith, declared, "This generation shall have my word through you" (D&C 5:10). There is, however, another explanation, one provided by the Savior himself on 19 January 1841: "Verily, verily, I say unto you, that when I give a commandment to any of the sons of men to do a work unto my name, and those sons of man go with all their might and with all they have to perform that work, and cease not their diligence, and their enemies come upon them and hinder them from performing that work, behold, it behooveth me to require that work no more at the hands of those sons of men, but to accept of their offerings. . . . Therefore, for this cause have I accepted the offerings of those whom I commanded to build up a city and a house unto my name, in Jackson county, Missouri, and were hindered by their enemies, saith the Lord your God" (D&C 124:49, 51).

Several times in our history statements have been made by Church members or leaders to the effect that individuals or groups would not taste of death before the second advent of the Lord Jesus Christ took place. Nevertheless, these individuals eventually died, and the Second Coming is yet to be. How do we explain this? The gift of prophecy, like all spiritual gifts, is one that requires wisdom and judgment and, to some extent at least, experience. It is one thing, for example, to receive a revelation from God, and another thing entirely to understand it. An individual may receive a great outpouring of peace in answer to a heartfelt petition for, let's say, a loved one who is suffering. Does the peaceful feeling mean the loved one will be made well? Does it mean that everything will work out as the petitioner desires? Or does it mean that the petitioner should take comfort and assurance that the right thing, the will of God, will take place?

Similarly, there have been times when men and women, overcome by the spirit of prophecy and revelation, have drawn conclusions from their spiritual experience that were not accurate. Some things in the future seemed closer than they really were. Elder Joseph Young, brother of President Brigham Young and one of the Presidents of the Seventy, explained that "the Holy Spirit brought many things close to [the early Saints'] minds—they appeared right by, and hence many were deceived, and [ran] into a mistake respecting them. They (the Saints) undertook to make calculations for to establish the kingdom and restore Israel, and many were so excited, that they wanted to take the Gospel from the Gentiles immediately. . . . Many good men made great blunders upon the subject of 'redeeming Israel.' . . . I knew that faith and the Holy Ghost brought the designs of Providence close by, and by that means we were enabled to scan them, and find out what they would produce when carried into effect, but we had not knowledge enough to digest and fully comprehend those things."[15]

12. How could a group claiming to be Christian deny blacks the priesthood for so long? What is the doctrinal basis for such a restriction?

Acting under divine direction, sometime late in the 1830s, the Prophet Joseph Smith established a policy that the blessings of the priesthood should be withheld from black members of The Church of Jesus Christ of Latter-day Saints. This practice continued in the Church through Joseph Smith's successors until President Spencer W. Kimball announced in June 1978 that a revelation had been received that all worthy males could receive the priesthood. We have no statement from Joseph Smith himself offering commentary or doctrinal explanation for such an action, though the record of the lineage-based granting or denial of priesthood anciently may be found in the scriptures (Moses 7:8, 22; Abraham 1:21–27; Genesis 4:1–15; Moses 5:18–41). Leaders of the Church have repeatedly affirmed that the position of the Church in regard to who does and does not bear the priesthood is a matter of revelation from heaven and not simply social or political expediency.

There is also scriptural precedent for restricting the full blessings of the gospel or the priesthood to certain individuals or groups of people. From the days of Moses to the coming of Jesus Christ, the Aaronic or Levitical Priesthood was conferred only upon worthy descendants of the tribe of Levi. In the first century after Christ, the message of salvation was presented first to the Jews (the "lost sheep of the house of Israel"; Matthew 10:6; 15:24) and then, primarily through the labors of the apostle Paul, to the Gentile nations. Ultimately the blessings of the Lord are for all people, "black and white, bond and free, male and female; and he remembereth the heathen; and all are alike unto God, both Jew and Gentile" (2 Nephi 26:33).

We do not know why the priesthood was withheld from

black Latter-day Saints for so long. We do know, however, that God has a plan, a divine timetable by which his purposes are brought to pass in and through his children on earth. He knows the end from the beginning and the times before appointed for specific doings and eventualities (Acts 17:26). That timetable may not be ignored, slighted, or altered by finite man. The faithful seek to live in harmony with God's will and go forward in life with all patience and faith.

13. Is it true that Latter-day Saint women occupy a second-class status in the Church? Why are they not ordained to the priesthood?

The leaders of the Church teach that men and women have roles in life that are equally important but different. Some roles are better suited to the masculine nature; others are more suited to the feminine. Women have natural and innate capacities to do some things that are more difficult for men, and vice versa. Because of the sanctity of the family and the home and because of the vital nature of the family in the preservation of society, we as Latter-day Saints teach that motherhood is the highest and holiest calling a woman can receive. We believe and teach that women should search, study, learn, prepare, and develop in every way possible—socially, intellectually, and spiritually—but no other role in society will bring as much fulfillment or contribute more to the good of humankind than motherhood.

Nothing in the doctrine of the Latter-day Saints suggests that men are preferred in the sight of God or that the Almighty loves males more than he loves females. Latter-day Saint doctrine condemns unrighteous dominion in any form (D&C 121:33–46), as well as any discrimination because of race, color, or gender (2 Nephi 26:33). God is no respecter of persons (Acts 10:34–35). Women are daughters of God, and they are entitled to every spiritual gift, every virtue, and every fruit of the Spirit. Priesthood is not maleness, nor should it be equated with male administration. A man who holds the priesthood does not have any advantage over a woman in qualifying for salvation in the highest heaven. Priesthood is divine authority given to worthy men, as a part of God's great plan of happiness. Why it is bestowed upon men and not upon women is not known. The highest ordinances of the priesthood, received in the temple, are given only to a man and a woman together.

Elder James E. Talmage stated: "In the restored Church of Jesus Christ, the Holy Priesthood is conferred, as an individual bestowal, upon men only, and this in accordance with Divine requirement. It is not given to woman to exercise the authority of the Priesthood independently; nevertheless, in the sacred endowments associated with the ordinances pertaining to the House of the Lord, woman shares with man the blessings of the Priesthood. When the frailties and imperfections of mortality are left behind, in the glorified state of the blessed hereafter, husband and wife will administer in their respective stations, seeing and understanding alike, and co-operating to the full in the government of their family kingdom. Then shall woman be recompensed in rich measure for all the injustice that womanhood has endured in mortality. Then shall woman reign by Divine right, a queen in the resplendent realm of her glorified state, even as exalted man shall stand, priest and king unto the Most High God. Mortal eye cannot see nor mind comprehend the beauty, glory, and majesty of a righteous woman made perfect in the celestial kingdom of God."[16]

14. What do the Latter-day Saints hope to accomplish in the world? What is the appeal of the Church?

Because we as Latter-day Saints are Christian, because we believe that peace and happiness here and hereafter are to be found only in and through Jesus Christ, we also believe that the only hope for the world is to come unto Christ. The answer to the world's problems—the vexing dilemmas of starvation, famine, disease, crime, inhumanity, and the dissolution of the nuclear family—is ultimately to be found not in more extravagant social programs or stronger legislation. We acknowledge and value the good that is done by so many to carry the message of the New Testament Jesus to a world that desperately needs it. At the same time, we say to a drifting world that there is more truth to be known, more power to be exercised, and more profound fulfillment to be had. As President Howard W. Hunter pointed out: "We seek to bring all truth together. We seek to enlarge the circle of love and understanding among all the people of the earth. Thus we strive to establish peace and happiness, not only within Christianity but among all mankind."[17]

The message of Mormonism is that there is a God; Jesus Christ is his divine Son; the Father and the Son have appeared and spoken again in these times; and the Father's plan of salvation has been restored to earth for the ultimate blessing of humankind. In short, the Latter-day Saints believe that God loves his children in this age and generation as much as he loved those to whom he sent his Son in person. The perfect love of God the Father is manifest not alone through the preservation of the biblical record but also through modern revelation, modern scripture, and modern apostles and prophets.

The Latter-day Saints offer hope to a world strangling with hopelessness. At a time when there is a waning of belonging, the Latter-day Saints invite all people to come home, to return to the family of God. If some of those who have wandered or lost their way can be reoriented toward their eternal possibilities, then Mormonism will have had a lasting effect on the world. The First Presidency of the Church in 1907 declared: "Our motives are not selfish; our purposes not petty and earth-bound; we contemplate the human race, past, present and yet to come, as immortal beings, for whose salvation it is our mission to labor; and to this work, broad as eternity and deep as the love of God, we devote ourselves, now, and forever."[18]

"No Unhallowed Hand"

In a day when men and women throughout the earth are leaving the faith of their parents and churches are closing down in ever-increasing numbers, The Church of Jesus Christ of Latter-day Saints continues to grow in an unprecedented manner. What is it about our faith, this system of salvation sometimes called Mormonism, that has such appeal to people throughout the earth?

For one thing, many in our day are weary of the shifting sands of secularity and the ever-mobile standards of society. They long for a return to time-honored values and absolute truths. Because wickedness is widening, honest truth seekers yearn for something to hold onto, something of substance, something that will stand when all else is falling. At the same time, they desire to be a part of a religious organization that requires something of them. In fact, recent sociological studies attest that the churches that are growing in our day are those that demand the most of their membership. In The Church of Jesus Christ of Latter-day Saints, for example, we do not apologize for our position on chastity and virtue, nor do we hesitate to teach the Word of Wisdom or the principle of paying tithes and offerings. We know that we remain steadfast and immovable in the faith to the degree that we invest ourselves in the faith.

Another significant appeal of the Church is our doctrine. It is comforting to know that God our Heavenly Father has a plan and that there is purpose to our struggles and suffering and even death. Consider the Latter-day Saint doctrine of life after death. The idea of a divine plan—including that which deals with the hereafter—is especially appealing to those who encounter Mormonism. "Expressions of the eternal nature of love and the hope for heavenly reunion," wrote Colleen McDannell and Bernhard Lang, "persist in contemporary Christianity. Such sentiments, however, are not situated within a theological structure. Hoping to meet one's family after death is a wish and not a theological argument. While most Christian clergy would not deny that wish, contemporary theologians are not interested in articulating the motif of meeting again in theological terms. The motifs of the modern heaven—eternal progress, love, and fluidity between earth and the other world—while acknowledged by pastors in their funeral sermons, are not fundamental to contemporary Christianity. Priests and pastors might tell families that they will meet their loved ones in heaven as a means of consolation, but contemporary thought does not support that belief as it did in the nineteenth century. There is no longer a strong theological commitment.

"The major exception to this caveat is the teaching of The Church of Jesus Christ of Latter-day Saints, whose members are frequently referred to as the Mormons. The modern perspective on heaven—emphasizing the nearness and similarity of the other world to our own and arguing for the eternal nature of love, family, progress, and work—finds its greatest proponent in Latter-day Saint (LDS) understanding of the afterlife. While most contemporary Christian groups neglect afterlife beliefs, what happens to people after they die is crucial to LDS teachings and rituals. Heavenly theology is the result not of mere speculation, but of revelation given to past and present church leaders." McDannell and Lange continued: "There has been . . . no alteration of the LDS understanding of the afterlife since its articulation by Joseph Smith. If anything, the Latter-day Saints in the twentieth century have become even bolder in their assertion of the importance of their heavenly theology. . . . In the light of what they perceive as a Christian world which has given up belief in heaven, many Latter-day Saints feel even more of a responsibility to define the meaning of death and eternal life."[1]

As we acknowledge that The Church of Jesus Christ of Latter-day Saints is a living and dynamic organization, one that responds to times and circumstances and needs—indeed, one that changes—we also rejoice in the absolute truths and eternal verities that anchor our faith and answer some of life's deepest questions. Those do not change, and they are taught in Latter-day Saint meetinghouses in Mobile and Milan, in Fairbanks and Frankfurt, in Spokane and São Paulo.

I participated recently in an interfaith dialogue with a wonderful professor of religion who happens also to be a Protestant minister. We spoke of our respective views of Jesus, focused on where we agreed, emphasized where we disagreed, and then entertained questions from the audience for half an hour or so. Throughout much of the evening my colleague and the members of the audience (most of whom were Protestant or Catholic) used again and again the phrase "traditional Christianity" to refer to what they believed, in contrast with what Latter-day Saints believed.

It occurred to me then how odd the phrase "traditional Christianity" is, as though there were some single, monolithic structure to which everyone else belongs except the Latter-day Saints, some universal church that enjoys universal agreement on matters doctrinal. Yet we know enough about present-day Christianity to know there is no such organization. Substantive theological differences between Evangelical Christians and Latter-day Saint Christians do exist, and though I have no desire whatever to minimize them, I am persuaded from very personal experience that the deeper we look into the core doctrines of our respective traditions, the more often we will find surprising similarities.

But even with our differences, does that require insurmountable walls to exist between us? Within the last while I have read a good deal about current Christian crises and doctrinal differences, including the inerrancy of scripture; whether God is completely sovereign over all things or whether God limits his control by allowing freedom of the will; whether God possesses a complete knowledge of the future; whether the Creation account is literal or figurative for how long it took to create the earth; the flood in the days of Noah was local or global; whether Christ was both fully God and fully human during his ministry or whether he relinquished his divinity for a season; whether only the predestined are saved or whether all have the potential for full salvation; whether individuals can indeed enjoy eternal security from the moment of their spiritual rebirth or whether they must endure faithfully to the end to have the hope of eternal life fully realized; the problem of evil; what happens to babies who die; whether baptism is essential to salvation and to whom it must be administered—infants or mature believers; whether the gifts of the Spirit ceased with the apostles or whether they can and should be enjoyed today; whether women should serve in certain ministerial capacities; the nature of the events leading up to the personal reign and ministry of Christ on earth; whether hell consists of eternal torment and suffering or whether those who reject Christ and his gospel are simply annihilated; whether man plays a role in his own salvation beyond an initial confession of Christ as Savior—the meaning and place of good works; whether one can accept Jesus as Savior but postpone until later a profession of Him as Lord and Master; psychological or social views of the Trinity; whether and how wives should submit to their husbands; and life after death.[2]

Some of these issues are significant. It seems to me that the divide between various evangelical groups on certain key issues is as great as the divide between evangelicals and Latter-day Saints. As the Prophet Joseph Smith observed: "If I esteem mankind to be in error, shall I bear them down? No. I will lift them up, and in their own way too, if I cannot persuade them my way is better; and I will not seek to compel any man to believe as I do, only by the force of reasoning, for truth will cut its own way. Do you believe in Jesus Christ and the Gospel of salvation which he revealed? So do I. Christians should cease wrangling and contending with each other, and cultivate the principles of union and friendship in their midst; and they will do it before the millennium can be ushered in and Christ takes possession of His kingdom."[3]

While no one is eager to be opposed or persecuted, while every person would like his or her religious convictions to be taken seriously, and while it would be so much more productive if people did not waste time and wear out their lives misrepresenting, insulting, or demeaning persons with differing religious views, we readily acknowledge that rabid opposition in many ways signals the truthfulness and significance of the work of The Church of Jesus Christ of Latter-day Saints. As Moroni predicted to the seventeen-year old Joseph Smith, "those who are not built upon the Rock will seek to overthrow this church; but it will increase the more opposed."[4]

Early in the history of the restored Church, Joseph Smith uttered a remarkable prophecy at the Morley Farm in Kirtland, Ohio. President Wilford Woodruff testified: "The Prophet said,

'Brethren, I have been very much edified and instructed in your testimonies here tonight, but I want to say to you before the Lord, that you know no more concerning the destinies of this Church and kingdom than a babe upon its mother's lap. You don't comprehend it.' I was rather surprised. He said 'it is only a little handfull of Priesthood you see here tonight, but this Church will fill North and South America—it will fill the world.'"[5]

President Boyd K. Packer declared: "Often we are asked how the relatively few Apostles in the First Presidency and the Twelve can manage the Church, now [in April 1999] more than 10 million strong.

"Actually the Church is no bigger than a ward. . . .

"No matter if the Church grows to be a hundred million (as it surely will!), it will still be no bigger than a ward. Everything needed for our redemption, save for the temple, is centered there—and temples now come ever closer to all of us."[6]

The Lord explained to his servant Joseph in 1831: "Verily, thus saith the Lord unto you—*there is no weapon that is formed against you shall prosper;* and if any man lift his voice against you he shall be confounded in mine own due time. Wherefore, keep my commandments; they are true and faithful" (D&C 71:9–11; emphasis added). The little stone cut out of the mountain without hands is rolling with accelerated force: the kingdom of God is going forth, all in preparation for that glorious kingdom of heaven yet to come (Daniel 2; D&C 65:2, 6). Like Peter of old, our gaze must not be affected by the winds and waves of adversity; our focus must ever be upon the Lord and our ears attuned to the witness and warning of his anointed servants. "For by doing these things," the Master assured the early Latter-day Saints, "the gates of hell shall not prevail against you; yea, and the Lord God will disperse the powers of darkness from before you, and cause the heavens to shake for your good, and his name's glory" (D&C 21:6).

Joseph Smith himself uttered the prophetic word in the Wentworth Letter that "the Standard of Truth has been erected; no unhallowed hand can stop the work from progressing; persecutions may rage, mobs may combine, armies may assemble, calumny may defame, but the truth of God will go forth boldly, nobly, and independent, till it has penetrated every continent, visited every clime, swept every country, and sounded in every ear, till the purposes of God shall be accomplished, and the Great Jehovah shall say the work is done."[7]

In the words of a modern apostle: "The Church is like a great caravan—organized, prepared, following an appointed course, with its captains of tens and captains of hundreds all in place.

"What does it matter if a few barking dogs snap at the heels of the weary travelers? Or that predators claim those few who fall by the way? The caravan moves on.

"Is there a ravine to cross, a miry mud hole to pull through, a steep grade to climb? So be it. The oxen are strong and the teamsters wise. The caravan moves on.

"Are there storms that rage along the way, floods that wash away the bridges, deserts to cross, and rivers to ford? Such is life in this fallen sphere. The caravan moves on.

"Ahead is the celestial city, the eternal Zion of our God, where all who maintain their position in the caravan shall find food and drink and rest. Thank God that the caravan moves on!"[8]

We need not fear for the future of the restored Church, and we certainly need not take counsel from such fears. My experience in working with good men and women of other faiths during the past decade teaches me that although there are those who will dislike us and condemn us no matter what we say or do, there are others—a growing number, to be sure—who recognize the fruits of our faith and who acknowledge our devotion to God and his Only Begotten Son. We have every reason to be optimistic, forward-looking, and confident as we anticipate the future.

Notes

INTRODUCTION
Don't Be Shocked

1. Proclamation of the Twelve Apostles, *Messages of the First Presidency,* 1:257.
2. Cannon, *Journal of Discourses,* 12:367.
3. Kimball, Conference Report, April 1981, 105.
4. Whitney, *Life of Heber C. Kimball,* 129–32; emphasis added.
5. Hinckley, Conference Report, October 1997, 92.
6. Hinckley, *Teachings of Gordon B. Hinckley,* 123–24.

CHAPTER 1
Reaching Out

1. Hunter, "The Gospel—A Global Faith," 18.
2. Hinckley, Conference Report, April 1998, 3.
3. Lewis, *Mere Christianity,* 178.
4. McConkie, Conference Report, October 1968, 135.
5. Grand Rapids, Mich.: Zondervan, 1997.
6. Whitney, Conference Report, April 1928, 59, as cited in Benson, Conference Report, April 1972, 49.
7. Roberts, Conference Report, April 1906, 15; emphasis added.
8. Boyd, *God of the Possible,* 17.
9. Boyd, *God of the Possible,* 130; see also Pinnock, *Most Moved Mover,* 65–111; Olson, *Story of Christian Theology,* 54–57.
10. Packer, Conference Report, April 2000, 7; paragraphing altered.
11. Smith, *Gospel Doctrine,* 31, 395, 399; see also Smith, *Journal of Discourses,* 15:325.

12. Roberts, Conference Report, April 1906, 14–15.
13. Maxwell, *Wherefore, Ye Must Press Forward,* 127.
14. Ballard, Conference Report, October 2001, 44–45.
15. Boyd, *God of the Possible,* 20.
16. Mouw, *Uncommon Decency,* 9.
17. Hinckley, as cited in Dew, *Go Forward with Faith,* 576.
18. Hinckley, Conference Report, April 1997, 116.
19. Hinckley, Conference Report, April 1998, 3.
20. Hinckley, Conference Report, April 1999, 116; see also April 2000, 110; April 2001, 4.
21. Hinckley, Conference Report, October 2001, 3–4.
22. Young, *Journal of Discourses,* 13:56; emphasis added.
23. Smith, *Teachings of the Prophet Joseph Smith,* 218.
24. Hunter, *That We Might Have Joy,* 59.

CHAPTER 2

How We Know

1. Whitney, *Life of Heber C. Kimball,* 446, 450.
2. Balmer, *Growing Pains,* 34, 61–62.
3. Blomberg, as cited in Strobel, *Case for Christ,* 52–53.
4. Maxwell, *Plain and Precious Things,* 4.
5. Benson, *A Witness and a Warning,* 13.
6. Benson, *A Witness and a Warning,* 31.
7. Hinckley, *Faith, the Essence of True Religion,* 10–11.
8. Packer, Conference Report, October 1985, 104, 107.
9. Young, *Journal of Discourses,* 8:355.
10. Nibley, *World and the Prophets,* 134.
11. McConkie, Conference Report, April 1971, 99.

CHAPTER 3

What Is Our Doctrine?

1. *Holman Bible Dictionary,* 374.
2. McConkie, *Mormon Doctrine,* 204.
3. Smith, *Teachings of the Prophet Joseph Smith,* 121.
4. Packer, Conference Report, April 1977, 80; emphasis added and paragraphing altered.

5. Packer, Conference Report, October 1986, 20.

6. Maxwell, *One More Strain of Praise,* x.

7. Hinckley, *Teachings of Gordon B. Hinckley,* 620.

8. Smith, *Teachings of the Prophet Joseph Smith,* 392.

9. Smith, *Gospel Doctrine,* 9.

10. Compare Smith, *Teachings of the Prophet Joseph Smith,* 9–10, 61, 327.

11. Smith, *Teachings of the Prophet Joseph Smith,* 278.

12. Smith, *Teachings of the Prophet Joseph Smith,* 268.

13. Snow, as cited in Maxwell, Conference Report, October 1984, 10.

14. Smith, *History of the Church,* 5:340.

15. McConkie, "Foolishness of Teaching," 12.

16. McKay, Conference Report, April 1907, 11–12; see also October 1912, 121; April 1962, 7.

17. Smith, *Teachings of the Prophet Joseph Smith,* 89.

18. McConkie, *Mormon Doctrine,* 608.

19. McConkie, "Are the General Authorities Human?"

20. Lee, *Teachings of Harold B. Lee,* 542.

21. Young, Kimball, and Wells, in *Messages of the First Presidency,* 2:232.

22. Hinckley, Conference Report, April 1992, 77.

23. Hinckley, "Continuing Pursuit of Truth," 5.

24. McConkie, "Gathering of Israel and the Return of Christ," 3, 5.

25. Smith, *Teachings of the Prophet Joseph Smith,* 24; see also D&C 93:33; 138:17.

26. Smith, *Teachings of the Prophet Joseph Smith,* 313.

27. Oaks, *Provo Daily Herald,* 21, as cited in Henderson, "A Time for Healing," 155–56.

28. McKay, Brown, and Tanner, First Presidency Message, January 1970.

29. McConkie, "New Revelation on Priesthood," 132.

30. Ballard, address at Elijah Abel Memorial Service, 2002.

31. Smith, *Teachings of the Prophet Joseph Smith,* 345–46.

32. Snow, *Teachings of Lorenzo Snow,* 1.

33. Smith, *Lectures on Faith,* 2:2.

34. Lee, *Teachings of Harold B. Lee,* 157.

35. Maxwell, Conference Report, April 1996, 94–95.

36. Maxwell, *Men and Women of Christ,* 2.

37. Personal correspondence, as cited in Matthews, "Using the Scriptures," 124.
38. Firmage, ed., *An Abundant Life: The Memoirs of Hugh B. Brown*, 124.
39. Maxwell, *That My Family Should Partake*, 87.
40. Maxwell, *All These Things Shall Give Thee Experience*, 4.

CHAPTER 4

WISDOM IN RESPONSE

1. Hinckley, Conference Report, April 2001, 4.
2. Shoemaker, "Why Your Neighbor Joined the Mormon Church," 11–13.
3. Ashton, Conference Report, April 1978, 9.
4. Smith, *From Prophet to Son*, 42–43.
5. Packer, *Teach Ye Diligently*, 62–63.
6. Packer, *Teach Ye Diligently*, chapter 11; Packer, *Holy Temple*, chapter 2.
7. Smith, *Teachings of the Prophet Joseph Smith*, 343.
8. *Clementine Recognitions*, III, 34, as cited in Nibley, *Since Cumorah*, 110; emphasis added.
9. Pratt, *Autobiography of Parley P. Pratt*, 298–99.
10. McKay, *Gospel Ideals*, 21–22.
11. McConkie, *Here We Stand*, 6; emphasis in the original.
12. Hinckley, Conference Report, October 1997, 92.

CHAPTER 5

THE SCRIPTURES

1. Smith, *Teachings of the Prophet Joseph Smith*, 56.
2. Smith, *Teachings of the Prophet Joseph Smith*, 61.
3. Smith, *Personal Writings of Joseph Smith*, 321–24; spelling and punctuation standardized.
4. Smith, *Teachings of the Prophet Joseph Smith*, 9–10, 61, 327.
5. Cannon, *Gospel Truth*, 472.
6. McGrath, *In the Beginning*, 300, 305.
7. Benson, Hinckley, and Monson, First Presidency Letter, 22 May 1992.
8. Packer, Conference Report, October 1982, 75.

9. Benson, *A Witness and a Warning,* 19–20.

10. Michael Whiting, as reported in "The Book of Mormon at the Bar of DNA 'Evidence,'" *Insights* 23, no. 2 (2003): 1, 4–5. See *Journal of Book of Mormon Studies* 12, number 1 (2003), a publication of the Foundation for Ancient Research and Mormon Studies (FARMS) at Brigham Young University, or write *Journal of Book of Mormon Studies,* P.O. Box 7113, University Station, Provo, Utah 84602. The email address is jbms@byu.edu, and the website is farms.byu.edu. Phone numbers are 801-422-9229 or 1-800-327-6715

11. Smith, *History of the Church,* 2:236.

12. Smith, *History of the Church,* 2:286.

13. Cowdery, *Latter-day Saints' Messenger and Advocate* 2 (1835): 236.

14. Anson Call Manuscript, 9, as cited in Call, "Anson Call and His Contributions," 33; emphasis added.

15. Taylor, *Times and Seasons* 4 (1 February 1843): 95; emphasis added.

16. Peterson, "History and Significance of the Book of Abraham," 2:173–74, citing Smith, *History of the Church,* 2:348.

17. McConkie, "Doctrinal Restoration," 21.

18. Oaks, "Scripture Reading and Revelation," 7.

19. Kimball, Conference Report, April 1977, 115.

20. McConkie, "New Commandment," 11.

CHAPTER 6

GOD AND MAN

1. *Cowley and Whitney on Doctrine,* 287.

2. See Paulsen, "Early Christian Belief," 105–16.

3. Kugel, *God of Old,* xii, 5–6, 63, 195; see also 81, 104–6, 134–35.

4. Pinnock, *Most Moved Mover,* 33–34.

5. Smith, *Teachings of the Prophet Joseph Smith,* 181.

6. Smith, *Teachings of the Prophet Joseph Smith,* 312.

7. McConkie, *New Witness for the Articles of Faith,* 61; see also 72–73.

8. Smith, *Doctrines of Salvation,* 1:12; see also McConkie, *Promised Messiah,* 166.

9. Robinson, "Eternities That Come and Go," 1.

10. Smith, *Lectures on Faith,* 5:2–3.
11. See Robinson, *Are Mormons Christians?* 60–61.
12. Lewis, *Mere Christianity,* 155; see also Lewis, *Weight of Glory,* 39–40.
13. Lewis, *Mere Christianity,* 176.
14. Pratt, *Key to the Science of Theology,* 21.
15. Hinckley, Conference Report, October 1994, 64.
16. Hatch, *Influence of Greek Ideas on Christianity,* 1, 4–5.
17. See Hopkins, *How Greek Philosophy Corrupted the Christian Concept of God,* especially 441–49.
18. Curran, "Creative Fidelity," 45.
19. From Celsus, *On the True Doctrine,* as cited in McConkie, *Sons and Daughters of God,* 108–9; emphasis added.
20. Boyd, *God of the Possible,* 17.
21. Boyd, *God of the Possible,* 130; see also Pinnock, *Most Moved Mover,* 65–111.
22. Pinnock et al., *Openness of God,* 9–10.
23. Erickson, *Making Sense of the Trinity,* 44.
24. Erickson, *Making Sense of the Trinity,* 46; emphasis added.
25. Rahner, *The Trinity,* 10–11.

CHAPTER 7

CHRIST AND SALVATION

1. Hinckley, Conference Report, October 2001, 3–4.
2. Hinckley, *Be Thou An Example,* 85–86.
3. Smith, *Gospel Doctrine,* 91.
4. Sperry, *Paul's Life and Letters,* 176.
5. Sperry, *Paul's Life and Letters,* 176.
6. Lewis, *Mere Christianity,* 131.
7. McConkie, *Doctrinal New Testament Commentary,* 2:499–500.
8. Oaks, Conference Report, October 1988, 78.
9. Smith, *Teachings of the Prophet Joseph Smith,* 12.
10. Stott, *Authentic Christianity,* 168.
11. Young, *Journal of Discourses,* 8:124–25; emphasis added.
12. Young, *Journal of Discourses,* 6:276.
13. Young, *Journal of Discourses,* 1:131.
14. McKay, *Gospel Ideals,* 6.
15. McKay, as cited in *Church News,* 28 February 1953.

16. Hinckley, *Teachings of Gordon B. Hinckley,* 636, 638, 623–24.
17. Church Educational System presentation on temples, as cited in Callister, *Infinite Atonement,* 294.
18. Callister, *Infinite Atonement,* 295.
19. Madsen, "The Temple and the Atonement," 72.
20. Talmage, *House of the Lord,* 84.
21. Callister, *Infinite Atonement,* 296.
22. Hinckley, *Teachings of Gordon B. Hinckley,* 635.
23. Hanks, "Christ Manifested to His People," 16; emphasis in original.
24. Cited in Robinson, *Are Mormons Christian?* 24–29.
25. Smith, *Sharing the Gospel with Others,* 12–13.

CHAPTER 8

JOSEPH SMITH AND CHURCH HISTORY

1. Anderson, "Parallel Prophets: Paul and Joseph Smith," 178–79.
2. Maxwell, Conference Report, October 1984, 12.
3. Cited in Backman, *American Religions and the Rise of Mormonism,* 181, 180.
4. Smith, *Teachings of the Prophet Joseph Smith,* 324.
5. Taylor, *Journal of Discourses,* 11:221.
6. Young, *Journal of Discourses,* 3:266.
7. See Pagels, *Adam, Eve, and the Serpent,* 11.
8. Pratt, *Journal of Discourses,* 1:63–64.
9. Hinckley, Conference Report, October 1998, 92.
10. Hinckley, Conference Report, October 1998, 92.
11. See Kimball, *Journal of Discourses,* 11:210.
12. Maxwell, *Things As They Really Are,* 46.
13. Smith, *Teachings of the Prophet Joseph Smith,* 256.
14. See McConkie, *Millennial Messiah,* 26–27, 405.
15. Young, *Journal of Discourses,* 9:230; emphasis added.
16. Talmage, "Eternity of Sex," 602–3.
17. Hunter, *That We Might Have Joy,* 59.
18. Smith, Winder, and Lund, First Presidency, Conference Report, April 1907, appendix, 16, as cited in Hunter, *That We Might Have Joy,* 59.

CONCLUSION

"NO UNHALLOWED HAND"

1. McDannell and Lange, *Heaven*, 312–13, 322.
2. See, for example, Boyd and Eddy, *Across the Spectrum;* Olsen, *Mosaic of Christian Belief;* Stackhouse, *Evangelical Landscapes.*
3. Smith, *Teachings of the Prophet Joseph Smith*, 313–14.
4. Oliver Cowdery, *Latter-day Saints' Messenger and Advocate* 2 (1835): 199.
5. Woodruff, Conference Report, April 1898, 57.
6. Packer, Conference Report, April 1999, 79.
7. Smith, *History of the Church*, 4:540.
8. McConkie, Conference Report, October 1984, 105.

Sources

Anderson, Richard Lloyd. "Parallel Prophets: Paul and Joseph Smith." *Speeches of the Year.* Provo, Utah: Brigham Young University, 1983.

Backman, Milton V. Jr. *American Religions and the Rise of Mormonism.* 2d ed. Salt Lake City: Deseret Book, 1970.

Ballard, M. Russell. *Church News,* 5 October 2002.

Balmer, Randall. *Growing Pains: Learning to Love My Father's Faith.* Grand Rapids, Mich.: Brazos Press, 2001.

Benson, Ezra Taft. *A Witness and a Warning: A Modern-Day Prophet Testifies of the Book of Mormon.* Salt Lake City: Deseret Book, 1988.

Benson, Ezra Taft, Gordon B. Hinckley, and Thomas S. Monson. First Presidency Message, 22 May 1992.

Blomberg, Craig. "Do the Biographies of Jesus Stand Up to Scrutiny?" In Lee Strobel, *The Case for Christ* (Grand Rapids, Mich.: Zondervan), 1998.

———. *How Wide the Divide?* Downer's Grove, Ill.: InterVarsity Press, 1997.

Boyd, Gregory A. *God of the Possible.* Grand Rapids, Mich.: Baker, 2000.

Boyd, Gregory A., and Paul R. Eddy. *Across the Spectrum: Understanding Issues in Evangelical Theology.* Grand Rapids, Mich.: Baker, 2002.

Brown, Hugh B. Personal correspondence with Robert J. Matthews, 28 January 1969, cited in Matthews, "Using the Scriptures," *Fireside and Devotional Speeches* (Provo, Utah: Brigham Young University), 1981.

Call, Duane D. "Anson Call and His Contributions toward Latter-day Saint Colonization." Unpublished master's thesis, Brigham Young University, 1956.

Callister, Tad R. *The Infinite Atonement.* Salt Lake City: Deseret Book, 2000.

Cannon, George Q. *Gospel Truth: Discourses and Writings of President George Q. Cannon.* 2 vols. in 1. Comp. Jerreld L. Newquist. Salt Lake City: Deseret Book, 1987.

Conference Report of The Church of Jesus Christ of Latter-day Saints. Salt Lake City: The Church of Jesus Christ of Latter-day Saints, April 1898; April 1906; April 1907; October 1912; April 1928; April 1962; April 1966; October 1968; April 1971; April 1972; April 1977; April 1978; April 1981; October 1982; October 1984; October 1985; October 1986; October 1988; April 1992; October 1994; April 1996; April 1997; October 1997; April 1998; October 1998; April 1999; April 2000; April 2001; October 2001; April 2002; October 2003.

Cowley and Whitney on Doctrine. Comp. Forace Green. Salt Lake City: Bookcraft, 1963.

Curran, Charles E. "Creative Fidelity: Keeping the Religion a Living Tradition." *Sunstone,* July 1987.

Dew, Sheri L. *Go Forward with Faith: The Biography of Gordon B. Hinckley.* Salt Lake City: Deseret Book, 1996.

Erickson, Millard. *Making Sense of the Trinity.* Grand Rapids, Mich.: Baker, 2000.

Firmage, Edwin B., ed. *An Abundant Life: The Memoirs of Hugh B. Brown.* Salt Lake City: Signature Books, 1988.

Hanks, Marion D. "Christ Manifested to His People." *Temples of the Ancient World: Ritual and Symbolism.* Ed. Donald W. Parry. Salt Lake City: Deseret Book and FARMS, 1994.

Hatch, Edwin. *The Influence of Greek Ideas on Christianity.* Gloucester, Mass.: Peter Smith Publishers, 1970.

Henderson, Juan. "A Time for Healing: Official Declaration 2." In *Out of Obscurity: The LDS Church in the Twentieth Century.* Salt Lake City: Deseret Book, 2000.

Hinckley, Gordon B. *Be Thou an Example.* Salt Lake City: Deseret Book, 1981.

———. "The Continuous Pursuit of Truth." *Ensign,* April 1986.

———. *Faith, the Essence of True Religion.* Salt Lake City: Deseret Book, 1989.

———. "Speaking Today: Excerpts from Recent Addresses from President Gordon B. Hinckley." *Ensign,* February 1998.

———. *Teachings of Gordon B. Hinckley*. Salt Lake City: Deseret Book, 1997.

Holman Bible Dictionary. Ed. Trent C. Butler. Nashville, Tenn.: Holman Bible Publishers, 1991.

Hopkins, Richard R. *How Greek Philosophy Corrupted the Christian Concept of God*. Bountiful, Utah: Horizon, 1998.

Hunter, Howard W. *That We Might Have Joy*. Salt Lake City: Deseret Book, 1994.

———. "The Gospel—A Global Faith." *Ensign*, November 1991.

Journal of Book of Mormon Studies 12, no. 1. Provo, Utah: Foundation for Ancient Research and Mormon Studies, 2003.

Journal of Discourses. 26 vols. London: Latter-day Saints' Book Depot, 1854–86.

Kugel, James L. *The God of Old: Inside the Lost World of the Bible*. New York: Free Press, 2003.

Latter-day Saints' Messenger and Advocate. Kirtland, Ohio: The Church of Jesus Christ of Latter-day Saints, 1834–37.

Lee, Harold B. *The Teachings of Harold B. Lee*. Ed. Clyde J. Williams. Salt Lake City: Bookcraft, 1996.

———. Unofficial transcript. LDS Student Association fireside. Utah State University, 10 October 1971.

Lewis, C. S. *Christian Reflections*. San Francisco: Harper Collins, 1967.

———. *Mere Christianity*. New York: Touchstone Books, 1996.

———. *The Weight of Glory*. New York: Touchstone, 1996.

Madsen, Truman G. "The Temple and the Atonement." *Temples of the Ancient World: Ritual and Symbolism*. Ed. Donald W. Parry. Salt Lake City: Deseret Book and FARMS, 1994.

Martin, Walter. *The New Cults*. Ventura, Calif.: Regal Books, 1980.

Maxwell, Neal A. *All These Things Shall Give Thee Experience*. Salt Lake City: Deseret Book, 1979.

———. *Men and Women of Christ*. Salt Lake City: Bookcraft, 1991.

———. *One More Strain of Praise*. Salt Lake City: Bookcraft, 1999.

———. *Plain and Precious Things*. Salt Lake City: Deseret Book, 1983.

———. *That My Family Should Partake*. Salt Lake City: Deseret Book, 1974.

———. *Things As They Really Are*. Salt Lake City: Deseret Book, 1978.

———. *Wherefore, Ye Must Press Forward*. Salt Lake City: Deseret Book, 1977.

McConkie, Bruce R. "Are the General Authorities Human?" Address delivered at the Institute of Religion, University of Utah, Salt Lake City, 28 October 1966.

———. *Doctrinal New Testament Commentary*. 3 vols. Salt Lake City: Bookcraft, 1965–73.

———. "The Doctrinal Restoration." In *The Joseph Smith Translation: The Restoration of Plain and Precious Things*. Ed. Monte S. Nyman and Robert L. Millet. Provo, Utah: BYU Religious Studies Center, 1985.

———. *The Foolishness of Teaching* [address to Church Educational System]. Salt Lake City: The Church of Jesus Christ of Latter-day Saints, 1981.

———. *The Millennial Messiah*. Salt Lake City: Deseret Book, 1982.

———. *Mormon Doctrine*. 2d ed. Salt Lake City: Bookcraft, 1966.

———. "A New Commandment: Save Thyself and Thy Kindred!" *Ensign*, August 1976.

———. "The New Revelation on Priesthood." In *Priesthood*. Salt Lake City: Deseret Book, 1981.

———. *A New Witness for the Articles of Faith*. Salt Lake City: Deseret Book, 1985.

———. *The Promised Messiah*. Salt Lake City: Deseret Book, 1978.

McConkie, Joseph Fielding. "The Gathering of Israel and the Return of Christ." Church Educational System Religious Educators' Symposium, August 1982, Brigham Young University, typescript.

———. *Here We Stand*. Salt Lake City: Deseret Book, 1995.

———. *Sons and Daughters of God*. Salt Lake City: Bookcraft, 1994.

McConkie, Joseph Fielding, and Robert L. Millet. *Sustaining and Defending the Faith*. Salt Lake City: Bookcraft, 1985.

McDannell, Colleen, and Bernhard Lange. *Heaven: A History*. New Haven: Yale University Press, 1988.

McGrath, Alister. *In the Beginning: The Story of the King James Bible and How It Changed a Nation, a Language, and a Culture*. New York: Anchor Books, 2001.

McKay, David O., Hugh B. Brown, N. Eldon Tanner. First Presidency Message, January 1970.

———. *Gospel Ideals*. Salt Lake City: Improvement Era, 1953.

———. *Church News*, 28 February 1953.

Messages of the First Presidency of The Church of Jesus Christ of Latter-day

Saints. Comp. James R. Clark. 6 vols. Salt Lake City: Bookcraft, 1965–75.

Millet, Robert L. *Grace Works.* Salt Lake City: Deseret Book, 2003.

———. *I Will Fear No Evil.* Salt Lake City: Bookcraft, 2002.

———. *The Mormon Faith: A New Look at Christianity.* Salt Lake City: Shadow Mountain, 1998.

———. "What Is Our Doctrine?" *Religious Educator* 4, no. 3 (2003).

———. "Outreach: Opening the Door or Giving Away the Store?" *Religious Educator* 4, no. 1 (2003).

Mouw, Richard J. *Uncommon Decency: Christian Civility in an Uncivil World.* Downers Grove, Ill.: InterVarsity Press, 1992.

Nibley, Hugh W. *Since Cumorah: The Book of Mormon in the Modern World.* Salt Lake City: Deseret Book, 1967.

———. *The World and the Prophets.* Salt Lake City: Deseret Book, and FARMS, 1987.

Oaks, Dallin H. *Provo Daily Herald,* 5 June 1988.

———. "Scripture Reading and Revelation." *Ensign,* January 1995.

Olson, Roger E. *The Mosaic of Christian Belief: Twenty Centuries of Unity and Diversity.* Downers Grove, Ill.: InterVarsity Press, 2002.

———. *The Story of Christian Theology.* Downers Grove, Ill.: InterVarsity Press, 1999.

Packer, Boyd K. *Teach Ye Diligently.* Salt Lake City: Deseret Book, 1975.

———. *The Holy Temple.* Salt Lake City: Bookcraft, 1980.

Pagels, Elaine. *Adam, Eve, and the Serpent.* New York: Random House, 1988.

Paulsen, David L. "The Doctrine of Divine Embodiment: Restoration, Judeo-Christian, and Philosophical Perspectives." *Brigham Young University Studies* 35, no. 4 (1996).

———. "Early Christian Belief in a Corporeal Deity: Origen and Augustine as Reluctant Witnesses." *Harvard Theological Review* 83, no. 2 (1990).

Penrose, Charles W. "Editor's Table." *Improvement Era,* September 1912.

Peterson, H. Donl. "The History and Significance of the Book of Abraham." In *The Pearl of Great Price.* Vol. 2 of *Studies in Scripture* series. Ed. Robert L. Millet and Kent P. Jackson. Salt Lake City: Randall Book, 1985.

Pinnock, Clark H. *Most Moved Mover: A Theology of God's Openness.* Grand Rapids, Mich.: Baker, 2001.

Pinnock, Clark H., Richard Rice, John Sanders, Williams Hasker, and David Basinger. *The Openness of God: A Biblical Challenge to the Traditional Understanding of God.* Downers Grove, Ill.: InterVarsity Press, 1994.

Pratt, Parley P. *Autobiography of Parley P. Pratt.* Salt Lake City: Deseret Book, 1976.

————. *Key to the Science of Theology.* Salt Lake City: Deseret Book, 1978.

Rahner, Karl. *The Trinity.* New York: Herder and Herder, 1970.

Robinson, Stephen E. *Are Mormons Christians?* Salt Lake City: Bookcraft, 1991.

————. "Eternities That Come and Go." *BYU Religious Studies Center Newsletter* 8, no. 3 (May 1994): 1.

Shoemaker, Donald P. "Why Your Neighbor Joined the Mormon Church." *Christianity Today,* 11 October 1974.

Smith, George Albert. *Sharing the Gospel with Others.* Comp. Preston Nibley. Salt Lake City: Deseret Book, 1948.

Smith, Joseph. *History of The Church of Jesus Christ of Latter-day Saints.* Ed. B. H. Roberts. 2d ed. rev. 7 vols. Salt Lake City: The Church of Jesus Christ of Latter-day Saints, 1932–51.

————. *Lectures on Faith.* Salt Lake City: Deseret Book, 1985.

————. *Personal Writings of Joseph Smith.* Ed. Dean C. Jessee. 2d ed. Salt Lake City: Deseret Book, 2002.

————. *Teachings of the Prophet Joseph Smith.* Sel. Joseph Fielding Smith. Salt Lake City: Deseret Book, 1976.

Smith, Joseph F. *From Prophet to Son: Advice of Joseph F. Smith to His Missionary Sons.* Comp. Hyrum M. Smith III and Scott G. Kenney. Salt Lake City: Deseret Book, 1981.

————. *Gospel Doctrine.* Salt Lake City: Deseret Book, 1971.

Smith, Joseph Fielding. *Doctrines of Salvation.* 3 vols. Comp. Bruce R. McConkie. Salt Lake City: Bookcraft, 1954–56.

Snow, Lorenzo. *The Teachings of Lorenzo Snow.* Ed. Clyde J. Williams. Salt Lake City: Bookcraft, 1996.

Sperry, Sidney B. *Paul's Life and Letters.* Salt Lake City: Bookcraft, 1955.

Stackhouse, John G., Jr. *Evangelical Landscapes: Facing Critical Issues of the Day.* Grand Rapids, Mich.: Baker, 2002.

————. *Humble Apologetics: Defending the Faith Today.* New York: Oxford University Press, 2002.

Stott, John. *Authentic Christianity.* Ed. Timothy Dudley-Smith. Downers Grove, Ill.: InterVarsity Press, 1995.

Talmage, James E. "The Eternity of Sex." *Young Woman's Journal,* October 1914.

————. *The House of the Lord.* Salt Lake City: Deseret Book, 1969.

Times and Seasons. 6 vols. Nauvoo, Ill.: The Church of Jesus Christ of Latter-day Saints, 1839–46.

Whitney, Orson F. *The Life of Heber C. Kimball.* Salt Lake City: Bookcraft, 1978.

Wilkins, Michael J., and J. P. Moreland, gen. eds. *Jesus under Fire.* Grand Rapids, Mich.: Zondervan, 1995.

INDEX